THE ALBION
On This Day

THE ALBION
On This Day

WEST BROMWICH
ALBION

*Baggies History, Facts & Figures
from Every Day of the Year*

DAVE BOWLER & LAURIE RAMPLING

THE ALBION
On This Day

History, Facts & Figures from Every Day of the Year

All statistics, facts and figures are correct as of 1st August 2009

© Dave Bowler and Laurie Rampling
Dave Bowler and Laurie Rampling have asserted their rights in accordance with
the Copyright, Designs and Patents Act 1988 to be identified as the authors of this work.

Published By:
Pitch Publishing (Brighton) Ltd
A2 Yeoman Gate
Yeoman Way
Durrington
BN13 3QZ

Email: info@pitchpublishing.co.uk
Web: www.pitchpublishing.co.uk

First published 2009

A catalogue record for this book is available from the British Library.

10-digit ISBN: 1-9054115-7-X
13-digit ISBN: 978-1-9054115-7-3

Printed and bound in Malta by Gutenberg Press

To Dad for taking me to the holy land so
often and to Mum for letting us go.

David Bowler

To my wife Marian for putting
up with an Albion fanatic!

To my sons, Mark, Darren and Stuart for
looking after their Mum when I wasn't around.

And finally to Dad, for
introducing me to the beautiful game.

Laurie Rampling

ACKNOWLEDGEMENTS

Thanks go to Albion historians and sages John Homer and Colin Mackenzie for helping to fill in a few of the blanks and confirm a few of the dates. Your help is much appreciated. May you find your reward in heaven, at three o'clock on a Saturday afternoon.

Thanks also to the following people and organisations for allowing use of their pictures: Paul Broadrick (p49), Joan Bowler collection (p77) and West Bromwich Albion's archive (p95, 105, 139, 159, 163). All other pictures are supplied by Laurie Rampling.

FOREWORD BY TONY BROWN

After making so many appearances and scoring a few goals for the Albion in my time at the club, I was delighted to be asked to write the foreword to this book.

I've been associated with the club since I came down from Manchester to join in 1961 after leaving school, and coming to the Albion was the best decision I ever made in my life. I made so many good friends here and had a wonderful career playing for some of the best supporters in the country. The fact that I still go to all the games to commentate is testimony to how the club got under my skin and how much I feel for it.

Looking through this book, it's amazing – and frightening! – just how many days in my life it brings back, and just how many other facts and stories I didn't know about my club. It's a great little read and I hope you enjoy reading it just as much as I have.

Tony Brown, West Bromwich Albion 1963-80

INTRODUCTION

Founded some 130 years ago, there were more than 47,000 days to choose from in the compilation of this day-by-day record of the evolution of West Bromwich Albion. Whittling a century and more worth of events down to a book you can hold in your hand rather than on a fork lift truck was some task.

From the controversial, to the record-breaking, to the historic, *On This Day* sees a host of greats flit across its pages, from the early pioneers such as Bassett and Pennington, through the legendary double winners of 1931 spearheaded by W. G. Richardson, to the great Ray Barlow and the Team of the Century in 1954; the Jeff Astle and Tony Brown double act of the 1960s, the Three Degrees from the 1970s and on to the successes of the new century with Jonathan Greening, Derek McInnes and Super Bob Taylor.

There are great names by the score here – alongside the less familiar – well known games rubbing up against the more surprising; wins next to defeats, trophies sitting with relegations. In the timeless words of Craig Shakespeare, "The slings and arrows of outrageous fortune" are all captured here; good times, bad times, the whole story.

Want to know what happened at The Hawthorns on your birthday, your wedding anniversary or just yesterday, or tomorrow, down the years? Then this is the place to look. *On This Day*, more happened than you might ever imagine...

Dave Bowler and Laurie Rampling, 2009

THE ALBION
On This Day

JANUARY

MONDAY 1st JANUARY 1979

Albion beat Bristol City in the first game of the Centenary Year. On an icebound pitch, Albion were able to get the game played by warming up in pimple-soled boots brought back from America where they were used on Astroturf in the NASL. The officials were impressed by Albion's ability to keep their footing and, thinking the surface was in better condition than it actually was, the game was played while most of the rest of the country saw games postponed. Albion strolled to a 3-1 win with two goals from Ally Brown and another from John Wile as City could barely keep their feet in their standard issue boots. City scored from a penalty which was retaken after Ally Brown was penalised for throwing a snowball as the original kick was struck.

SATURDAY 2nd JANUARY 1943

A wartime day best forgotten on the football field as an Albion team filled with guest players slumped to a 9-0 defeat away at Leicester City.

MONDAY 2nd JANUARY 1978

Under the caretaker management of playing colleague John Wile, Tony Brown registered his 250th goal for the club, still the only Albion man to reach that mark in senior games. Bomber achieved the tally by snatching a late equaliser as the Throstles grabbed a 2-2 draw at Chelsea's Stamford Bridge. Ally Brown scored the other goal in front of a 30,302 crowd.

MONDAY 3rd JANUARY 1983

Albion posted their highest attendance of the season, be it home or away, as they drew 0-0 at Manchester United's Old Trafford in front of 39,123 supporters. In a season of poor crowds across the board, the next best were 38,208 as Albion lost 2-1 at Tottenham Hotspur in the FA Cup fourth round, and 35,652 on the opening day as Albion were beaten 2-0 at Liverpool. The best home crowd of the season had come back in October – 25,331 for the local derby with Aston Villa – as the Baggies won 1-0 thanks to a Nicky Cross goal. The average gate of 15,260 at The Hawthorns was the lowest since 1914/15.

ALLY BROWN SCORED TWICE IN THE SNOW AGAINST BRISTOL CITY ON 1ST JANUARY 1979

SATURDAY 4TH JANUARY 1958

The FA Cup campaign opened in resounding style as the Baggies beat Manchester City 5-1 at The Hawthorns. A crowd of 49,669 paid £7,500 to see a brace from Ronnie Allen, an own goal by Ewing and strikes from Frank Griffin and Ray Barlow to round out the emphatic win.

SATURDAY 5TH JANUARY 1946

Len Millard made his 'official' debut in the 1-1 FA Cup draw at Cardiff's Ninian Park. In the first, and so far only, year where these ties were played over two legs, Albion triumphed 4-0 in the return, before losing out in the next round to the eventual cup winners, Derby County. Millard had joined Albion as an amateur in May 1937 and made his debut in a wartime game against Northampton on August 29th 1942, going on to skipper the side in later years.

SATURDAY 5TH JANUARY 1991

A day that will live on in infamy as the Baggies were conclusively beaten 4-2 at home by non-league Woking, Albion having even scored the first goal of the game. That failed to settle the nerves and Woking's Tim Buzaglo claimed the headlines with a hat-trick, while the fallout from defeat saw Brian Talbot lose his job as manager, replaced initially by Stuart Pearson as caretaker boss and then by former Albion striker Bobby Gould.

SATURDAY 5TH JANUARY 2002

Hoards of Albion supporters headed north to Wearside for an early kick-off at Sunderland's Stadium of Light in a third round FA Cup tie. Jason Roberts turned in a virtuoso display to run the Sunderland defence ragged as the Baggies beat their Premier League opponents 2-1 with goals from Neil Clement and Andy Johnson.

SATURDAY 6TH JANUARY 1973

Tony Brown clocked up his 400th first team appearance for the Throstles, but there was little to celebrate as Albion crashed 3-0 to Sheffield United at Bramall Lane. It began a catastrophic sequence where Albion took just five points from a dozen games to plummet towards relegation from the First Division.

SATURDAY 6TH JANUARY 1990

The Baggies beat First Division Wimbledon in a third round FA Cup tie at The Hawthorns with Gary Robson and Kevin Bartlett scoring the goals that ended the Crazy Gang's hopes of repeating their 1988 FA Cup Final triumph.

SATURDAY 7TH JANUARY 1888

Four goals from Jem Bayliss were more than enough to see Albion through their fifth round FA Cup tie with Stoke City in a 4-1 win at the Stoney Lane ground. Contrary to popular belief, Albion have defeated Stoke since then, but, sadly, not very often.

SATURDAY 7TH JANUARY 1961

Albion were on the wrong end of a nasty FA Cup shock as they were beaten 3-1 at Lincoln City. Andy Graver scored a hat-trick for the Imps with David Burnside getting the consolation goal for the top flight side. Among other shocks, Blackpool were thrashed 6-2 by Scunthorpe United and Crewe beat Chelsea 2-1 at Stamford Bridge.

FRIDAY 8TH JANUARY 1971

Doug Fraser, who had skippered Albion in the League Cup final at Wembley less than 12 months earlier, left the club, joining Nottingham Forest for £40,000. Fraser, who had joined Albion from his native Aberdeen in 1963, played a total of 325 games for the Baggies and won cup winner's medals in both the League Cup (1966) and the FA Cup (1968). Utterly unaware of where West Bromwich was when he first signed, on his first morning in the Black Country, he surprised the hotel reception staff by asking them, "Where's the beach?"

TUESDAY 8TH JANUARY 1980

The Throstles were beaten 2-1 at Upton Park in a third round FA Cup replay, West Ham United going on to win the cup that year by beating Arsenal at Wembley with a Trevor Brooking header. Tony Brown came on as a substitute for Albion and scored the last goal of his senior career at the club, number 279. The West Ham side included former Baggie David Cross who went on to claim the only FA Cup winner's medal of his career.

SATURDAY 9TH JANUARY 1915

Albion slipped to a surprise 1-0 defeat at Hull City in the first round of the FA Cup. It was to be Albion's last FA Cup game for five years and a day because of World War I. When the FA Cup resumed after the Armistice, the Baggies fared no better, losing in the first round at home to Barnsley by the only goal, the only blot on the otherwise immaculate title-winning season.

SATURDAY 9TH JANUARY 1926

Albion took their place in the third round of the FA Cup in the first season where both First and Second Division sides were made exempt from the two opening rounds. Albion took advantage of the situation by beating Bristol City 4-1 with two goals from Tommy Glidden and one each from Jack Byers and Joe Carter in the tie at The Hawthorns.

SATURDAY 9TH JANUARY 1937

Goalkeeper Harold Pearson made his last appearance for the Baggies in a 5-3 defeat at Portsmouth's Fratton Park, Harry Jones and W. G. Richardson (2) getting Albion's goals. Pearson's departure for Millwall brought an end to the Pearson goalkeeping dynasty at The Hawthorns which had started way back in February 1906 when his dad, Hubert, first joined the club. Harold succeeded him between the sticks in 1927. Between them, over the course of their two careers, they won the league championship, FA Cup, promotion and an England cap.

SATURDAY 9TH JANUARY 1954

The FA Cup-winning campaign of 1953/54 got underway in low-key fashion as the Throstles squeezed past Chelsea by a single goal at The Hawthorns. The future West Ham United and England boss Ron Greenwood scored the only goal of the game – in his own net.

SATURDAY 10TH JANUARY 1953

Albion recorded a 4-1 win over West Ham United at Upton Park in the third round of the FA Cup, George Lee, Paddy Ryan, Ronnie Allen and Johnnie Nicholls scoring the goals that saw them through in front of a crowd of 35,150 that paid £4,676.

WEDNESDAY 11TH JANUARY 1939

The Baggies were in imperious form as they trounced Manchester United 5-1 in a third round FA Cup replay at Old Trafford after a goalless draw in West Bromwich. Harry Jones got two goals, Doug Witcomb, Ike Clarke and W. G. Richardson got the others, the latter's being his last ever FA Cup goal for the club, bringing his tally to 26, a number only bettered by Tony Brown with 27. Albion were beaten 2-0 by the eventual cup winners Portsmouth in round four, their last FA Cup tie before the outbreak of World War II.

SATURDAY 11TH JANUARY 1947

Ray Barlow and Dave Walsh were on the mark with the important goals as Leeds United were seen off in the third round of the FA Cup, 2-1, earning Albion a tie with Charlton Athletic in the fourth round which they promptly lost – 2-1.

SATURDAY 12TH JANUARY 1963

Albion's was the only game to survive the big freeze which wiped out the rest of the Football League programme and decimated the football season through the first two months of the year. The Throstles called on supporters and officials to help clear snow from the pitch, an effort that brought the dubious reward of a 3-0 defeat at the hands of Sheffield Wednesday. Just 15,710 spectators braved the icy conditions to watch the game, further evidence that they should have left the snow where it was.

SATURDAY 12TH JANUARY 1974

Tony Brown underlined his liking for the teams from the East Midlands by scoring all four of Albion's goals in the 4-1 win over Nottingham Forest at the City Ground. Seven days earlier, the Bomber had scored a hat-trick against Notts County in the 4-0 FA Cup win at The Hawthorns.

THURSDAY 12TH JANUARY 1978

Ronald Franklin Atkinson was appointed Albion's new manager in succession to Ronnie Allen. Atkinson joined the club from Cambridge United, then leading the promotion race in Division Three. Colin Addison, who was also interviewed for the position was named as his assistant.

SATURDAY 13TH JANUARY 1912

Albion began their FA Cup campaign by comfortably disposing of Tottenham Hotspur, 3-0, with goals by Syd Bowser, Charlie Deacey and Harry Wright in front of 21,947 fans. It was to be a gruelling season in the cup as Albion played eight games all told before they finally lost by the only goal to Barnsley in the FA Cup final replay.

SATURDAY 13TH JANUARY 1973

One of the most long-winded FA Cup ties in Albion's history commenced in innocuous enough fashion as the Baggies played out a 1-1 draw on home soil against Nottingham Forest. The replay at the City Ground saw the teams locked at 1-1 (Hartford scoring for Albion) when the game was abandoned due to thick fog. The teams tried again at Forest's ground, only to end up at 0-0 after extra time. The deadlock was finally broken at the fourth attempt when goals from Len Cantello, Hartford and Colin Suggett saw the Throstles through 3-1 at Leicester's Filbert Street after 379 minutes of football. Albion were eventually knocked out by Leeds United in the fifth round, Leeds going on to lose to Sunderland in one of the biggest upsets in FA Cup history.

SATURDAY 13TH JANUARY 1979

A Cyrille Regis goal earned Albion a 1-1 draw at Norwich City and put the Baggies on top of the top division, a feat they have not repeated since. David Mills appeared as an unused substitute having just joined the club for £516,000 from Middlesbrough, which was then a British record transfer fee. Albion's progress was then hampered by freezing winter weather which saw them play just one First Division fixture in the next six weeks, away at Anfield where they lost 2-1 to the eventual champions Liverpool who continued to play regularly courtesy of their undersoil heating.

SATURDAY 13TH JANUARY 1996

Alan Buckley's team ended their record-breaking run of 11 straight league defeats by drawing 0-0 with Wolves at The Hawthorns, while also contriving to miss a penalty. The team quickly got back to losing ways though, losing two more in succession after this brief respite.

SATURDAY 14TH JANUARY 1961

Clive Clark made his debut for the Baggies in a 3-1 win over Preston North End at The Hawthorns, Alec Jackson scoring twice to add to a Don Howe penalty. Clark went on to become a hero amongst the Albion support, his thrilling wing play following in the post war tradition of the likes of George Lee, Frank Griffin and Billy Elliott.

SATURDAY 15TH JANUARY 1944

Both Billy Elliott and Horace Ball scored hat-tricks as Albion hammered Walsall 7-1 at The Hawthorns in the qualifying round of the wartime Football League Cup. Doug Whitcomb got the other goal in front of 4,800 people, who paid £340 for the privilege of having a brief break from thoughts of the war.

SUNDAY 15TH JANUARY 2006

An epic Sunday lunchtime in Lancashire ended with Albion reigniting their survival bid at the bottom of the Premier League by beating Wigan Athletic at the JJB Stadium. Darren Moore was dismissed for a professional foul, Martin Albrechtsen ran half the length of the field to score a rare Albion goal and in the final seconds, goalkeeper Tomasz Kuszczak produced what was named the BBC's 'Save of the Season' to deny Jason Roberts – a save reminiscent of Gordon Banks' stop from Pele in the 1970 World Cup.

TUESDAY 15TH JANUARY 2008

The Baggies twice threw away the lead in the third round FA Cup replay with Charlton Athletic, taking the game into extra time before ending 2-2, Roman Bednar and James Morrison scoring for the home side. Albion finally made progress into the next round by winning 4-3 on penalties, Roman Bednar scoring the crucial penalty in front of the Smethwick End.

THURSDAY 15TH JANUARY 2009

Marc-Antoine Fortune joined the Baggies on loan until the end of the season, moving across the Channel from Nancy to take up his role up front. Fortune scored five goals by the end of the season but was unable to save Albion from relegation back to the Championship.

SATURDAY 16TH JANUARY 1937

Albion dumped non-league Spennymoor out of the FA Cup with a 7-1 win in the third round. Teddy Sandford and W. G. Richardson both scored twice, Wood, Mahon and Jones finishing the scoring. The Throstles made it all the way to the FA Cup semi-final before losing to Preston North End.

SATURDAY 16TH JANUARY 1954

The Throstles remained top of the pile in the First Division after a Ronnie Allen goal was enough to beat Tottenham Hotspur at White Hart Lane.

SATURDAY 16TH JANUARY 1993

Ossie Ardiles' team won their first away league game in nearly three months to get their promotion challenge back on track, goals from Heggs, Hackett and an Ian Hamilton penalty beating Exeter City 3-2.

SATURDAY 17TH JANUARY 1920

Albion's relentless march to the league title continued unimpeded with a 5-2 thrashing of Blackburn Rovers, Magee, Bentley, Morris, Crisp and Gregory all helping themselves to a goal. In the previous league game, the Baggies had won 5-1 – at Blackburn's Ewood Park ground. Alf Bentley had notched a hat-trick on that occasion.

WEDNESDAY 17TH JANUARY 1934

Albion lost 1-0 at home to Chelsea in a third round replay. Jack Sankey made his Albion debut in the first game at Stamford Bridge and went on to play 290 games for the club, scoring 27 goals, achieving the rare distinction of playing in every position including goalkeeper when he deputised for the injured Harold Pearson in an FA Cup tie at Hull in January 1936 as Albion won 2-0.

SATURDAY 17TH JANUARY 2009

The Throstles completed a first ever Premier League double by beating Middlesbrough 3-0, following up the 1-0 win earlier in the season at the Riverside. It was also the first time Albion had ever won three successive home games in the Premiership, following on from the wins over Tottenham Hotspur and Manchester City.

SATURDAY 18TH JANUARY 1902

Albion collected their tenth straight league win, to post a record that remains intact more than a century later. Burslem Port Vale were the tenth victims as the Baggies won 3-2 having already beaten Burton 3-1 (a), Lincoln 4-1 (h), Middlesbrough 2-0 (h), Barnsley 3-1 (h), Stockport County 3-0 (h), Leicester Fosse 3-0 (a), Preston North End 2-1 (a), Leicester Fosse again 1-0 (h) and Burnley 3-0 (h). Gainsborough Trinity ruined the sequence by grabbing a draw before the Throstles then reeled off another five wins in a row on their way to winning the Second Division by four points from Middlesbrough.

SATURDAY 18TH JANUARY 1936

The Throstles smashed Blackburn Rovers 8-1 at The Hawthorns in front of a crowd of 16,434. W. G. Richardson knocked in a hat-trick, as did Jack Mahon; Jack Sankey and Walter Robbins bagged a goal apiece. They followed that by beating Liverpool 6-1 in the next league fixture but these were rare moments of cheer in a season where Albion won only 16 games out of 42 and finished 18th – ahead of both Liverpool and bottom-placed Blackburn.

SATURDAY 18TH JANUARY 2003

Despite losing Igor Balis to injury after 35 minutes and having Andy Johnson sent off 16 minutes from time, the Throstles managed to eke out a 0-0 draw at Leeds United's Elland Road to breathe hope into the fight against relegation in the first Premier League season.

SATURDAY 19TH JANUARY 1889

The inaugural league derby game against Aston Villa ended in defeat for Albion, losing 2-0 at Villa Park in front of a reported crowd of 10,000. Albion restored some pride seven days later when they held Villa to a 3-3 draw on home soil.

SATURDAY 19TH JANUARY 1952

Despite being 3-0 down with just 14 minutes left, Albion fight back to get a 3-3 draw against Charlton Athletic at The Valley in a Division One game, scoring three in nine minutes through George Lee, Ronnie Allen and Frank Griffin.

SATURDAY 19TH JANUARY 2002

One of the club's greatest heroes, Jeff Astle, passed away in Burton-upon-Trent. Perhaps no loss since that of Billy Bassett nearly 65 years before had so affected the Albion family and almost as soon as the announcement was made, fans were leaving flowers, scarves and shirts at The Hawthorns in tribute to the King. In the wake of his death, the Astle Gates were erected in his memory at the Birmingham Road entrance to the stadium.

SUNDAY 20TH JANUARY 2002

Albion defeated Walsall 1-0 in a Division One game, supporters of both sides having first immaculately respected a minute's silence in memory of Jeff Astle who had passed away the previous day. On scoring the only goal of the game, Jason Roberts removed his shirt to reveal an Astle T-shirt beneath in tribute to the great number nine.

SATURDAY 20TH JANUARY 2007

Despite losing an early goal, the Throstles bounced back to win 3-2 at Elland Road, goals from Jonathan Greening and two from Dio Kamara doing the trick. The game ended amid a spiteful atmosphere with Leeds boss Dennis Wise ordered from his technical area by the referee.

SATURDAY 21ST JANUARY 1899

Blackburn Rovers were put to the sword by a rampant Albion outfit who romped to a 6-2 win at Stoney Lane, Flewitt and McKenzie both scoring twice, Bassett and Garfeld adding the other goals.

SATURDAY 21ST JANUARY 1928

Jimmy Cookson scored four as Albion beat Reading 5-3 at The Hawthorns, an Inglis own goal completing the scoring. Cookson went on to score 38 goals that season, a record that stood until W. G. Richardson surpassed it in 1935/36.

SATURDAY 21ST JANUARY 2006

Defeat against the all but doomed Sunderland, 1-0 at The Hawthorns, ensured Albion were embroiled in the relegation battle. Sunderland were without a win in 14 league games when they pitched up in the Black Country but the Black Cats were good value for their win against the Baggies who were booed off at the end.

SATURDAY 22ND JANUARY 1983

A Peter Eastoe goal was the only strike of a game against West Ham United at Upton Park. The win was the only one amid a sequence of 12 games which saw a promising start under Ron Wylie's management peter out. The victory in London was followed by five straight draws, four of them 0-0.

SATURDAY 22ND JANUARY 2005

A fully deserved 2-0 win over Manchester City with goals from Kevin Campbell and the Player of the Year, Ronnie Wallwork, set Albion off on the trail of the 'Great Escape' as they climbed off the bottom of the table to avoid relegation at the season's end. It was only the second league win of the campaign and Bryan Robson's first victory as manager in 12 attempts, though he had previously seen Albion come through an FA Cup tie at Preston North End's Deepdale.

SATURDAY 23RD JANUARY 1886

In a game which neatly represented the changing football times – from the days of the public school amateurs to the new professionalism of the fast approaching Football League – Albion beat the Old Carthusians by a single Green goal in a fifth round FA Cup tie. Old Westminsters were beaten in the next round as Albion marched on to the FA Cup final where they were eventually beaten by Blackburn Rovers.

SATURDAY 23RD JANUARY 1943

Aston Villa were well beaten, 5-3, at Villa Park in a qualifying round of the wartime Football League Cup. Under wartime rules, which allowed players to guest for other clubs, Irish international Peter Doherty starred for the stripes, scoring twice, Billy Elliott, Charles Evans and Tom Green getting the other goals.

SATURDAY 23RD JANUARY 1971

Ipswich Town came to The Hawthorns and held Albion to a 1-1 draw in the fourth round of the FA Cup, Colin Suggett scoring for the home team. The Baggies were beaten 3-0 in the replay and with league form patchy at best, cup failure hastened the end of the Alan Ashman era at the end of the season.

SATURDAY 24TH JANUARY 1931

A tight FA Cup tie at White Hart Lane was decided in Albion's favour when Stan Wood scored the only goal of the game to send the Baggies into round five of the competition. Wood's goal kept them in the hunt for the unique double of winning both FA Cup and promotion in the same season, a prize that was duly won at the end of the season.

FRIDAY 24TH JANUARY 1964

While reversing his car out of his parking space at Albion's Spring Road training ground, manager Jimmy Hagan drove it over the edge of a bank and into the canal below. Players dashed to rescue the manager from the car, only to find that he had already kicked the windscreen out and was getting out of the car under his own steam. After they'd helped him out of the water, several players then carried him up the bank to safety. Noting they were breathing heavily as they did so, the disciplinarian manager concluded they weren't fit enough and ordered extra training in the afternoon.

SATURDAY 25TH JANUARY 1958

In a rollercoaster FA Cup fourth round tie at The Hawthorns, the Throstles recovered from a goal down to Nottingham Forest to lead 3-1 – only to end up drawing 3-3. Albion's three goals came between the 63rd and 67th minutes, scored by Bobby Robson, Derek Kevan and Ronnie Allen. Albion were successful in the replay, then beat Sheffield United, again in a replay, before their cup run was halted at Old Trafford in another replay amid the outpouring of emotion following the loss of the Busby Babes in the Munich air disaster.

SATURDAY 25TH JANUARY 1992

What was statistically the worst season in Albion history – the Baggies finished seventh in Division Three – ground miserably onwards as Swansea City visited The Hawthorns, immersed in their own fight against relegation, but returned to Wales with all three points. The Throstles were beaten 3-2 despite two goals from Graham Roberts, one of those from the penalty spot. A crowd figure of just 10,395 told its own story.

SATURDAY 26TH JANUARY 1935

Sheffield United were on the receiving end of a 7-1 thumping at The Hawthorns in a fourth round FA Cup tie. W. G. Richardson grabbed a hat-trick, Teddy Sandford scored twice, and Joe Carter and Arthur Gale finished the rout. The Steel City had the last laugh over the Throstles that season though as Sheffield Wednesday beat Albion in the Wembley final, 4-2.

WEDNESDAY 27TH JANUARY 1869

William Isaiah Bassett was born in West Bromwich. Bassett went on to be one of the greatest names in the history of the football club, winning the FA Cup, being named team captain and then, after hanging up his boots, becoming a director and chairman of the Albion. In his playing prime, he also represented England as a speedy winger on 16 occasions, scoring seven times for his country. As an Albion player, Bassett racked up 311 games and scored 77 goals, remarkable figures given the professional game was in its infancy when he was in his prime.

SUNDAY 27TH JANUARY 1974

For the first time, Albion played an FA Cup game on a Sunday afternoon. Football was allowed on the Sabbath as midweek evening games were outlawed, the impact of the miners' strike and the three-day week ensuring that floodlit football was severely reduced. The Sunday service was a roaring success as 53,509 worshippers packed Everton's Goodison Park to watch the Baggies get a 0-0 draw in the fourth round game. Albion won the replay back in the Black Country thanks to a Tony Brown goal.

SATURDAY 27TH JANUARY 1990

In torrential rain and on a saturated pitch, the Throstles defeated First Division Charlton Athletic in a fourth round FA Cup tie. The only goal of the match was scored by Tony Ford, the only outfield player to have played over 1,000 competitive games in English football. Quite regularly through the 90 minutes, it seemed as if the game would have to be called off as the ball got stuck in standing water, but the contest was seen through to its conclusion and delivered up a thrilling, and sometimes comical, spectacle for 18,172 soaking punters.

TUESDAY 28TH JANUARY 1958

In spite of seeing Maurice Setters stretchered off in the days before substitutes were allowed, the Throstles won 5-1 in an FA Cup fourth round replay at Nottingham Forest. A crowd of 46,455 saw Kevan, Whitehouse, Griffin, Robson and Howe score the goals that took Albion through.

SUNDAY 28TH JANUARY 2007

Few FA Cup ties have been so eagerly anticipated, nor enjoyed with such relish, as this fourth round tie which took Albion to Molineux. Because of FA regulations over ticket allocation, the Albion support was granted the entire stand behind the goal and the supporters made the absolute most of their day as the Throstles shredded on their own patch of Staffordshire, goals from Dio Kamara and Kevin Phillips either side of half time setting up victory before Zoltan Gera added salt to the wound with a late third, somersaulting in celebration in front of the Albion fans. The supporters left a reminder of their presence at the ground, covering the orange seats with Tesco carrier bags, reference to the home fans' derogatory chant about Albion's kit.

SATURDAY 29TH JANUARY 1927

Albion secured only their second win in 12 games when two goals from Stan Davies and another from Joe Carter were enough to beat Bury 3-1, though by that stage, the Baggies were already in deep trouble at the bottom of the First Division. They were ultimately relegated from the top flight, bottom of the division just seven years after they had been crowned as the record-breaking champions of England.

SATURDAY 29TH JANUARY 1972

The Baggies set off on a run of three successive wins, and five out of seven, that took them away from trouble at the bottom of the First Division, by beating Manchester United 2-1 in front of a huge crowd of 46,992 at The Hawthorns. Bobby Gould and Jeff Astle were the goalscorers on the day, the first time Don Howe's twin strike force had both scored in the same game, Astle managing just four goals all season as a string of knee injuries began to take their toll.

ZOLTAN GERA'S TRADEMARK SOMERSAULT AFTER SCORING IN THE 3-0 WIN OVER WOLVES ON 28TH JANUARY 2007

SATURDAY 30TH JANUARY 1937

County Durham-born W. G. Richardson smashed an FA Cup hat-trick to put down a feisty challenge from Darlington, cup fighters from his native north-east, the Baggies coming through 3-2. The hat-trick was his second and last for Albion in the FA Cup. W. G. had already shown a liking for opponents from his part of the world, scoring twice in the 7-1 demolition of Spennymoor United in the third round.

SATURDAY 30TH JANUARY 1954

The post-war attendance boom saw an impressive crowd of 48,242 people pack The Hawthorns as Albion completed a comfortable fourth round FA Cup win over Rotherham United on the way to Wembley. Johnnie Nicholls scored twice and Ronnie Allen and Paddy Ryan also got among the goals in a 4-0 win.

FRIDAY 31ST JANUARY 1969

Dennis Clarke, who became the first substitute to be used in an FA Cup final when he replaced John Kaye for extra time in 1968, was sold to Huddersfield Town for £20,000. The transfer saga had actually begun back in early May 1968, before the final itself, but took several months to come to its conclusion. Clarke's days were numbered when Ray Wilson emerged as the natural successor to Graham Williams in the wake of the 1968 triumph.

TUESDAY 31ST JANUARY 2006

After Albion played out a hard fought 0-0 draw at Charlton Athletic, Nigel Quashie underwent a medical in the Valley's away dressing room before signing for the Baggies from Southampton for a fee in the region of £1million, a switch which made the David Mills purchase back in 1979 look like the buy of the century. It would be true to say that Quashie was not a success at The Hawthorns, but he certainly enjoyed a lively start – Man of the Match on debut in a win over Blackburn Rovers, anonymous in game two, a 6-1 thrashing at Fulham, before he then picked up a well deserved straight red card and a three game ban in his third match against Middlesbrough. Quashie played just 30 times for Albion before moving on to West Ham United for another seven-figure sum.

THE ALBION
On This Day

FEBRUARY

SATURDAY 1st FEBRUARY 1890

Albion thrashed Burton Wanderers 23-0 in the first round of the Staffordshire Cup. Billy Bassett scored six goals, one of just ten occasions in the history of the Albion that a player has registered a double hat-trick for the first team. Pearson, Woodbine, Evans and Perry were all on half shift and scored three apiece, Wilson scored a brace, while Horton, Roberts and Green chimed in with a goal each in the rout.

WEDNESDAY 1st FEBRUARY 1967

In their first season in European competition, Albion were given a lesson in the realities of the game on the Continent. They were beaten in comprehensive fashion by Bologna in Italy with West German World Cup star Helmut Haller outstanding as the home team strolled to a 3-0 first leg win in the third round of the Inter-Cities Fairs Cup.

SATURDAY 1st FEBRUARY 1992

Having joined the Baggies from Bristol City for a fee of around £300,000, 'Super' Bob Taylor made his Albion debut against Brentford at The Hawthorns in a Third Division game, scoring in a 2-0 win in front of 15,984 supporters. Wayne Fereday got the other goal.

MONDAY 2nd FEBRUARY 1953

Vic Buckingham was appointed the Albion's new manager in the wake of Jesse Carver's departure to Valdagno, leaving Bradford Park Avenue to take the job and staying in the post until June 18th 1959. Buckingham led Albion to the 1954 FA Cup triumph when the club also finished second in Division One. Buckingham was a member of the elegant 'push and run' side that had won the First Division for Tottenham Hotspur in 1950/51, and he brought that Continental approach to The Hawthorns. Albion were widely proclaimed for playing the most progressive football in the country; one pundit even suggested they should represent England en masse at the 1954 World Cup finals.

MONDAY 2nd FEBRUARY 1981

Tony Brown played his final first team game at The Hawthorns, coming on for the last 27 minutes of a friendly against Red Star Belgrade. Albion won 4-2 in front of a crowd of 3,217.

SATURDAY 3rd FEBRUARY 1962

A red letter day in the capital city as the Baggies recorded a rare win at Highbury, Albion victorious 1-0 over Arsenal thanks to a goal from Clive Clark. It was only the second away win of the season, the first having come at St. Andrew's when Birmingham City were beaten 2-1 back in the previous September.

WEDNESDAY 3rd FEBRUARY 1982

The Throstles were held to a goalless draw by Tottenham Hotspur in the first leg of the League Cup semi-final at The Hawthorns, the Baggies unable to breach a solid defensive barrier erected by Keith Burkinshaw's team. Hopes of reaching a first Wembley final since the League Cup were ended by defeat at White Hart Lane seven days later when a goal from Hazard sent Spurs through instead.

SUNDAY 3rd FEBRUARY 2002

Albion produced a superb away display in front of the TV cameras to defeat Burnley 2-0 at Turf Moor. Jason Roberts was in especially irresistible form, scoring twice and taking the Clarets to the cleaners, picking up some rough treatment from the home defence before he was substituted with the game won.

SATURDAY 4th FEBRUARY 1888

George 'Spry' Woodhall scored on his England debut against Wales in a 5-1 win at Crewe. His only other cap came a month later on 17th March when he was involved in the 5-0 win over Scotland at Hampden Park.

THURSDAY 4th FEBRUARY 1937

Albion's worst ever league defeat was inflicted on them by Stoke City as they crashed to a 10-3 beating before a crowd of 15,230. W. G. Richardson, Wally Boyes and Walter Robbins got the goals that weren't much consolation.

TUESDAY 4th FEBRUARY 1997

A late comeback saw Albion, 2-1 down with 12 minutes left, beat Birmingham City 3-2 at St. Andrew's, Richard Sneekes scoring the equaliser. Bob Taylor grabbed his second goal of the game to win it in injury time.

SATURDAY 5TH FEBRUARY 1966

In freezing cold weather, the Throstles warmed the crowd up with a 5-3 win over Nottingham Forest, Clive Clark, John Kaye, Tony Brown, Bobby Hope and Bobby Cram scoring the goals. The win came just days after Albion had been soundly battered at Upton Park, 4-0, by West Ham United, their forthcoming opponents in the two-legged League Cup final in March, and represented an important boost for morale after the Throstles had struggled through a miserable January of three defeats and a draw from five fixtures.

SATURDAY 5TH FEBRUARY 2005

Kieran Richardson made his full debut for the Baggies at Norwich City and gave the first indication of how important he would be to Albion's hopes of survival with a driving display from the middle of the park and a debut goal to boot. Despite dominating the game, Albion were beaten 3-2, putting their hopes of survival in real doubt.

SATURDAY 6TH FEBRUARY 1926

The Throstles posted a resounding victory at home to Birmingham City, George James scoring two and Charlie 'Tug' Wilson putting three past the hapless Blues defenders as Albion marched to a 5-1 win in front of 23,104.

WEDNESDAY 6TH FEBRUARY 1952

Albion, drawn away to Gateshead in the FA Cup, won 2-0 after the game was switched to Newcastle United's ground for safety reasons. Ronnie Allen got both goals, the crowd totalling 38,681, considerably more than could have watched the tie at Gateshead's own home.

THURSDAY 6TH FEBRUARY 1997

Ray Harford was appointed Albion manager in succession to Alan Buckley, giving him time to use the rest of a meandering campaign to take stock of the players he had at his disposal. Among his key signings in his brief stint in charge were Lee Hughes, Alan Miller and Kevin Kilbane; he also appointed Cyrille Regis to his coaching team. Harford remained at The Hawthorns until December 4th 1997 when he walked out to join QPR as boss, leaving Albion in a strong position in Division One after a good start to the season.

SATURDAY 7TH FEBRUARY 1981

Bryan Robson scored his famous back-heel goal, captured by the *Match of the Day* cameras, as Albion beat Liverpool 2-0, Cyrille Regis scoring the other goal. Albion finished fourth that season while Bob Paisley's team ended in fifth spot – the last time the Baggies finished above Liverpool in the league table.

SATURDAY 8TH FEBRUARY 1958

Albion fought back from 2-1 down to win 3-2 against Nottingham Forest at The Hawthorns. Derek Kevan registered a brace and Bobby Robson scored the other goal as the Baggies looked to keep up with the pacesetters at the top of the First Division.

WEDNESDAY 8TH FEBRUARY 1967

A 2-2 draw at Upton Park saw Albion through to their second successive League Cup final, this one to be held at Wembley Stadium rather than over two legs as in the previous season. Bobby Hope and Clive Clark scored in London, but the real damage had been done in the first leg when the Baggies went one better than in the final of the year before, again scoring four against the Hammers, but this time without replay. A Jeff Astle hat-trick and another from Hope put Albion on easy street going into the second leg. Third Division Queens Park Rangers would be the final opponents, the Throstles red hot favourites to retain the trophy they had won at the first attempt in 1966.

SATURDAY 8TH FEBRUARY 2003

A late equaliser from Andy Johnson gave the Baggies a 1-1 draw against fellow strugglers Bolton Wanderers at the foot of the Premier League. In a typically all-action afternoon, Johnson came on as a substitute, broke his foot, scored a goal and bared his rear end to a steward in celebration. Just another day for Andy Johnson...

SATURDAY 9TH FEBRUARY 1901

The Hawthorns staged its first ever FA Cup tie as the Throstles beat Manchester City 1-0 with a Ben Garfield goal. The game was initially scheduled for January 26th 1901 but the weather forced a postponement.

SUNDAY 9TH FEBRUARY 1958

Legendary Albion goalscorer Cyrille Regis was born in Maripiasoula, French Guyana. He came to England to grow up in the London area, where he was spotted by Ronnie Allen "putting the ball, goalkeeper and two defenders into the net". Allen told a sceptical Albion board that if they would not stump up the money to buy Regis – around £5,000 – he would do it himself and they could pay him back once big Cyrille had made the grade.

SATURDAY 10TH FEBRUARY 1962

Albion thrashed Bolton Wanderers 6-2 with Derek Kevan and Keith Smith both scoring twice, Bobby Hope and Stuart Williams added the other goals.

SATURDAY 10TH FEBRUARY 1968

Asa Hartford made his debut for the Baggies in a 1-1 draw against Sheffield United at Bramall Lane, Jeff Astle getting Albion's goal. Hartford was only 17 at the time of his debut but went on to make a further five appearances in the cup winning season and admitted he was disappointed not to play at Wembley in the showpiece game. By the following season, Hartford was an established regular for the Throstles.

SATURDAY 10TH FEBRUARY 1973

Len Cantello played his 100th Albion game in an otherwise forgettable fixture as Albion were soundly beaten 4-0 by Crystal Palace at The Hawthorns on the way to relegation.

SATURDAY 11TH FEBRUARY 1893

A couple of goals from Billy Bassett were enough to see off Stoke City in a First Division fixture, Albion avenging an early season reverse against their nemesis.

SATURDAY 11TH FEBRUARY 1956

Charlton Athletic smashed Albion 5-1 at The Valley, Johnnie Nicholls scoring Albion's only goal of the game in front of a slim crowd of 13,573. The once prolific Nicholls was in sad decline by then and scored just three more goals before the end of an Albion career that had flared so memorably into life back in the 1953/54 season.

SATURDAY 12TH FEBRUARY 1887

On their way to a second successive FA Cup final, the Albion defeated Lockwood Brothers in a fifth round tie, Green and Paddock getting the goals in a 2-1 score. This was Albion's second victory in the same tie, the first result have being rendered null and void after they had won 1-0 thanks to a 'Spry' Woodhall goal. The game was ordered to be replayed by the Football Association following a protest about the Woodhall goal. The replay took place at Derby County, Albion emerging victorious.

WEDNESDAY 12TH FEBRUARY 1969

A total of 45,348 fans watched Albion win a fifth round FA Cup tie, beating Arsenal 1-0 at The Hawthorns, Tony Brown scoring the only goal of the game. The FA Cup holders remained on course for a successful defence of their title. Their sixth round opponents were another side from London, Albion charged with the task of going to Stamford Bridge to take on Chelsea.

SATURDAY 13TH FEBRUARY 1915

Albion's game at Oldham Athletic's Boundary Park was abandoned because of a sudden blizzard after 27 minutes, the visitors a goal to the good thanks to Freddie Morris' strike. The restaged fixture took place on March 9th 1915 ended up as a 1-1 draw, John Crisp scoring.

SATURDAY 13TH FEBRUARY 1982

In an FA Cup fifth round tie, Cyrille Regis collected a ball out of defence from Alistair Robertson in the centre circle, turned, advanced into Norwich City territory and from 35 yards out, unleashed an unstoppable drive into the top corner to win the Goal of the Season award from the BBC's *Match of the Day*. There was no further scoring, nor was there any need after that one.

TUESDAY 13TH FEBRUARY 2007

Goals from Paul McShane and Dio Kamara gave the Throstles a 2-1 win over Colchester United to prolong a period of fine league form that eventually extended to taking 19 points out of 21 as Albion continued to push for promotion from the Championship under Tony Mowbray.

SATURDAY 14TH FEBRUARY 1903

Harry Hadley made his one and only England appearance, against Ireland at Molineux. England went on to claim a very straightforward victory, beating their visitors 4-0.

SUNDAY 14TH FEBRUARY 1986

A St. Valentine's Day massacre began with the appointment of Ron Saunders as manager. He dismantled the side in the following 18 months, his transfer dealings especially unsuccessful, at least in hindsight. In a single stroke, he set Albion back several years and saved the Wolves by selling Steve Bull to the Molineux club, but there were other contentious departures too, while the style of football did not meet with the taste of Albion supporters. Saunders was eventually sacked on September 1st 1987. Saunders was boss for 67 games, winning just 14 of them.

TUESDAY 15TH FEBRUARY 1916

Lt. Harold Godfrey Bache was killed in action in France whilst serving with the Lancashire Fusiliers. He had joined Albion in 1914, playing 14 times and scoring four goals. Prior to joining the Throstles, Bache was an amateur international for England – winning seven caps – and he also played cricket for Worcestershire. Bache's name lives on, however, inscribed forever on the Menin Gate memorial in Ypres.

SATURDAY 15TH FEBRUARY 1958

Ronnie Allen got Albion a draw with his goal in an FA Cup fifth round game at Sheffield United, watched by 55,847 fans. The Baggies won the replay 4-1, in spite of Frank Griffin breaking his leg during the course of the game. Griffin was never the same player again and his career at the top level was effectively finished.

SATURDAY 15TH FEBRUARY 1997

Paul Peschisolido scored a hat-trick and Richard Sneekes added another as Albion gave Ray Harford his first win as manager in a 4-2 victory at Norwich City's Carrow Road to ease any lingering worries about relegation. Peschisolido added a second hat-trick for the club the following season and the Canadian international was a prolific scorer for the Throstles in his brief stay, registering 21 goals in 41 starts and 10 substitute appearances.

SATURDAY 16TH FEBRUARY 1935

Albion swatted Stockport aside in the fifth round of the FA Cup, winning 5-0 up at Edgeley Park, W. G. Richardson getting two goals, Joe Carter, Arthur Gale and Wally Boyes weighing in with the rest. Even so, it was still a bit of a come down from the fourth round where the Baggies had thrashed Sheffield United 7-1, W. G. netting a hat-trick in that particular fixture.

SATURDAY 16TH FEBRUARY 2008

Coventry City were given very short shrift at the Ricoh Arena as the Baggies dismantled them in a fifth round FA Cup tie, the 5-0 scoreline a fair reflection of Albion dominance. Chris Brunt scored early on before a brace from Roman Bednar and other goals from Ishmael Miller and Zoltan Gera completed another hammering of the Sky Blues.

SATURDAY 17TH FEBRUARY 1962

Interest in the FA Cup was ended for another year with a 4-2 defeat at home to eventual winners Tottenham Hotspur. At least the Baggies had dumped Wolves out of the competition in the previous round.

SATURDAY 17TH FEBRUARY 1968

The Baggies suffered a setback in their FA Cup run as they were held at home by Southampton, Tony Brown scoring for Albion in the 1-1 draw.

SATURDAY 17TH FEBRUARY 1979

As England suffered in the big freeze that was to cost Albion the title, Ron Atkinson took his side to Guernsey for training and to play a friendly against Birmingham City on a local parks pitch, Cyrille Regis scoring in the 1-1 draw.

SATURDAY 17TH FEBRUARY 1990

Gary Robson suffered a broken leg as Albion slipped to a 2-0 defeat in the FA Cup at home to Aston Villa. Brother Bryan sustained broken legs in two separate incidents at The Hawthorns in 1976/77. Although Gary stayed with the Albion until the end of the 1992/93 campaign, this injury was really the beginning of the end of his time at The Hawthorns.

SATURDAY 18TH FEBRUARY 1928

Wolverhampton Wanderers were the visitors at The Hawthorns and were promptly sent packing after the Throstles inflicted a 4-0 thrashing on their local rivals in front of a crowd of 37,342. Jimmy Cookson led the way with two goals, Joe Carter and Charlie 'Tug' Wilson adding the others. Albion were in vintage goalscoring mood at the time, rattling in 21 goals in the course of six Division Two games early in 1928, yet they could still only finish 8th in the table.

SATURDAY 18TH FEBRUARY 1967

Not a vintage FA Cup year as the Baggies crashed out in the fourth round, suffering their heaviest defeat in the competition, a 5-0 beating at Don Revie's Leeds United. It was the fifth consecutive season where the Throstles had failed to progress beyond round four in the competition, but they did go on to make amends the following year.

SATURDAY 18TH FEBRUARY 1984

Johnny Giles returned for his first game of his second stint as Albion manager, but the omens were not good as the Throstles slumped to a 1-0 home defeat at the hands of Plymouth Argyle, of the Third Division, in the fifth round of the FA Cup. Sadly, it was the sign of things to come under Giles' leadership.

SATURDAY 19TH FEBRUARY 1921

The great goalscorer Bobby Blood scored a penalty on his debut in the 3-1 win over Tottenham Hotspur at The Hawthorns, Bentley and Crisp getting the others. Blood wasn't with the Albion for long, but he made a real impression, thumping in 26 goals in 53 games.

SATURDAY 19TH FEBRUARY 2000

It was becoming increasingly clear that Brian Little's reign as the manager at The Hawthorns was coming towards its final days as the Baggies were beaten out of sight at Sheffield United's Bramall Lane. The home side won 6-0 on a disastrous day for the Albion, Richard Sneekes also being sent off as the side continued to plummet down the First Division table.

SATURDAY 20TH FEBRUARY 1897

William 'Billy' Williams – an early inspiration for Harry Enfield's Charles 'Charlie' Charles perhaps? – was a stylish full-back who won his first England cap against Ireland in Nottingham in a 6-0 win. He won five further caps for his country, England winning every game in which he played including the remarkable 13-2 victory over Ireland at Roker Park on February 18th 1899.

SATURDAY 20TH FEBRUARY 1993

The Osvaldo Ardiles philosophy of "If they score five, we'll score six" came undone in a fixture at Stockport County where Albion's bid for automatic promotion from Division Two was derailed as the Baggies slumped to a 5-1 defeat, Bob Taylor getting Albion's goal.

WEDNESDAY 21ST FEBRUARY 1968

In an intense atmosphere at The Dell, Southampton, the Baggies came through a testing fourth round FA Cup replay 3-2 winners with two from Jeff Astle and another from Tony Brown. Goalkeeper John Osborne came off injured at the break, diminutive skipper Graham Williams going in goal and, despite having lit cigarette ends and coins flicked at him from behind the goal, he kept the Saints at bay to see Albion through.

MONDAY 21ST FEBRUARY 1921

Albion's players made a pilgrimage to the Cenotaph in Whitehall to lay a wreath in memory of their colleague Harold Bache who was killed in action in Flanders on February 15th 1916. Many members of the playing staff such as Sid Bowser, Claude Jephcott, Alf Bentley, Hubert Pearson and Jesse Pennington had lined up in the same Albion side as Bache in the 1914/15 season, while many others had served in various units on the home front or in combat zones overseas during the Great War, and were only too well aware how fortunate they were to still be playing football.

SATURDAY 21ST FEBRUARY 2004

Having fallen behind at Bramall Lane, Albion recovered late on to clinch three crucial promotion points against Sheffield United, central defenders Thomas Gaardsoe and Darren Moore coming up with the goals that turned the game around.

SATURDAY 22ND FEBRUARY 1930

Jimmy Cookson carried on his merry way towards a season's total of 33 league goals by poaching two more in the 4-2 win over Bradford City at The Hawthorns. Joe Carter and Tommy Glidden rounded out the goalscoring for the day in front of a poor crowd of just 11,770.

SATURDAY 22ND FEBRUARY 1936

Heavy snow saw the Throstles' game with local rivals Aston Villa abandoned after 26 minutes with Albion a goal to the good through Teddy Sandford. 39,111 disappointed fans were sent home from The Hawthorns. The fixture was replayed on April 1st – Albion were beaten 3-0.

SATURDAY 23RD FEBRUARY 1889

Albion played the final game of the inaugural Football League season, signing off with a 1-0 win at Everton, Fred Crabtree scoring the only goal in his one and only league appearance for the club which, at least, gave him a 100% goalscoring record. Albion finished sixth out of 12 at season's end with 22 points from 22 games. Preston North End were the first champions, running up 40 points, while Stoke propped up the table with just 12.

SATURDAY 23RD FEBRUARY 1952

Wolverhampton-born Johnnie Nicholls made his Albion debut in the FA Cup fifth round tie at Blackburn Rovers as Albion slipped to a single goal defeat. Nicholls scored 64 goals in 145 games for the club.

SATURDAY 23RD FEBRUARY 1957

Luton Town found themselves on the wrong end of an emphatic beating as the Baggies scored four times without reply, Jimmy Dudley, Brian Whitehouse, Frank Griffin and Derek Kevan all helping themselves to goals as the Hatters were put to the sword.

MONDAY 23RD FEBRUARY 1981

Tony Brown played his last game in Albion colours, playing the first 45 minutes of the centenary game between Albion and Poole. The Baggies beat the home side 4-2. Brown then left the club to finish his senior career with Torquay United.

SATURDAY 24TH FEBRUARY 1894

In their first ever group match in the United Counties League, Albion travelled to Small Heath – later to become Birmingham City – and came away with an epic 5-4 win, Pearson and McLeod both managing to score twice with Geddes adding the other goal. Albion repeated the victory at Stoney Lane in the return fixture two days later, winning 3-1 on their way to topping the group that also included Stoke City (5-0 at home, 2-5 away) and Wolverhampton Wanderers (2-4 away, 3-1 at home). Albion eventually met Derby County in the final, a game which ended in a draw. The replay was not held until the following season, Albion losing 3-1.

SATURDAY 24TH FEBRUARY 1906

A team long since lost to the Football League, Glossop, were heavily defeated by a rampant Albion outfit, the visitors savaged to the tune of six goals to nil. 'Chippy' Simmons scored twice, the other goals shared by 'Cock' Pheasant, Bruce Rankin, Eli Bradley and Adam Hayward.

SATURDAY 24TH FEBRUARY 1940

Because of bomb damage at St. Andrew's, Albion's away game against Birmingham City in the wartime Regional League was staged at The Hawthorns. The Throstles took full advantage of the territorial switch, winning 6-1.

WEDNESDAY 25TH FEBRUARY 1920

Two goals from Alf Bentley were enough to see off Manchester United at Old Trafford in a 2-1 win as the Throstles tightened their stranglehold at the top of the First Division table on their way to the title. This was the ninth win in ten games, a sequence that broke the back of the challengers and set Albion up to win the Championship in some style.

SATURDAY 25TH FEBRUARY 1967

Eddie Colquhoun made his Albion debut in a 2-2 draw against Sunderland at The Hawthorns, Fraser and Astle scoring the goals. Colquhoun had his Albion career disrupted by injury the following season and, by the time he was fit again, John Kaye had been converted from centre-forward to centre-half and kept him out of the side.

TUESDAY 26TH FEBRUARY 1991

The managerial reign of Bobby Gould began at The Hawthorns, a spell of 69 games which saw Albion relegated to the third tier of English football for the first time, while the crowd became disenchanted with the essentially 'route one' approach the side took to their football, in direct opposition to the club's traditions as a footballing side. Gould was relieved of his duties after Albion failed to win promotion in his only full season at the helm.

SATURDAY 26TH FEBRUARY 1994

Albion headed into Staffordshire to take on promotion-chasing Wolves, the Baggies having their own worries to occupy them at the other end of the table. Goals from Bob Taylor and Paul Mardon – better known to the supporters as 'Captain Mardon – International!' – saw the Albion to a memorable win, 2-1.

SATURDAY 27TH FEBRUARY 1926

Club stalwart Bob Finch made his first team debut as Albion beat Leicester City at The Hawthorns, winning 3-1. In spite of playing some 245 games for the Albion, Finch was perhaps as well known in his role as captain of the club's reserves through the early 1930s as they took a hat-trick of Central League titles from 1932/33 to 1934/35, Finch having also been in the Central League winning team of 1926/27. Finch never scored for the Baggies' first team, and was unfortunate enough to miss out on both the Wembley appearances of 1931 and 1935.

SATURDAY 27TH FEBRUARY 1937

Albion became embroiled in an extraordinary game with Sunderland at The Hawthorns, the Throstles eventually coming out on top in a ten-goal classic, winning 6-4. W. G. Richardson, Wally Boyes, Lawrence Coen, Cecil Shaw with a penalty and two goals from Harry 'Popeye' Jones saw the Albion prepare in fine fashion for the followings week's sixth round FA Cup tie with Arsenal.

SATURDAY 27TH FEBRUARY 1965

Aston Villa were beaten 3-1 at The Hawthorns, a Bobby Cram penalty adding to goals from Jeff Astle and Bobby Hope as the Throstles completed the double over the men from Witton.

SATURDAY 28th FEBRUARY 1891

Hopes of another FA Cup final were dashed by Blackburn Rovers who put Albion out of the competition at the semi-final stage with a 3-2 win in Stoke, the third time that Rovers had defeated the Baggies in seven seasons in the competition.

TUESDAY 28th FEBRUARY 1905

The club accounts showed a huge loss of £861 15s 9d over nine months, leading to an Extraordinary General Meeting of shareholders during which the entire Board, led by chairman Jem Bayliss, resigned. A new Board was duly elected on March 6th, comprising Harold Walker, Enoch Wood, Charles Couse, T. H. Spencer, W. Baker and Billy Bassett. They elected Mr. H. Keys as chairman, beginning the club's gradual recovery from the depths of despair.

WEDNESDAY 28th FEBRUARY 1973

Albion upset the odds to beat Arsenal 1-0 at The Hawthorns, Tony Brown scoring the only goal of the game as struggling Albion ended a sequence of four straight defeats, inflicting serious damage on the Gunners' title hopes in the process. The Baggies then went seven more games without a win to doom the club to relegation.

TUESDAY 28th FEBRUARY 1978

Tony Brown collected his 200th league goal in the 2-1 win over Birmingham City at St. Andrew's, only the third Albion man to do so, after W. G. Richardson and Ronnie Allen. Ally Brown got the other goal of the game as Blues were beaten.

MONDAY 29th FEBRUARY 1892

Albion beat Wednesbury Old Athletic 4-0 in the semi-final of the Dudley Charity Cup at Stoney Lane, Perry (2), Geddes and Groves the scorers.

SATURDAY 29th FEBRUARY 1964

Clive Clark, John Kaye and Ronnie Fenton got the goals that beat Wolves 3-1 at The Hawthorns, just 19,829 turned out to see the rare leap year fixture, a reflection of the mediocre seasons that both teams were enduring as they struggled to recapture the glories of the previous decade.

THE ALBION
On This Day

WEST BROMWICH ALBION

MARCH

SATURDAY 1st MARCH 1969

In the 'Battle of the Bridge', Albion won 2-1 at Chelsea in the sixth round of the FA Cup, the game ending in a punch up as John Osborne made a last minute save by sitting on the ball, Chelsea players trying to kick it from beneath him. Tony Brown missed a penalty but scored along with Astle to win the game, with many who were there numbering this as amongst the finest performances ever given by an Albion side. Sadly, they could not recapture that level of form in the next round and they lost the semi-final to Leicester City.

SATURDAY 2nd MARCH 1889

Albion posted their record FA Cup win by beating Chatham 10-1 away with three goals from 'Tug' Wilson, two each from Billy Bassett and Jem Bayliss, Charlie Perry and George Timmins scoring once each to add to an own goal. Regular foes Preston North End stopped Albion's charge in the semi-final, gaining revenge for the defeat Albion had inflicted on them in the previous year's final.

THURSDAY 2nd MARCH 1950

One of the club's all-time greats, Ronnie Allen, signed for the Throstles from Port Vale for £18,000 and made his debut two days later, scoring in the 1-1 draw against Wolverhampton Wanderers in front of a crowd of 60,945. Allen struggled to get in the ground on the day of the match, the doorman not believing his claim that he was a player. He was a player alright! Allen went on to score 234 senior goals for the Albion, 208 of them in the league, both records until they were surpassed by Tony Brown.

SATURDAY 2nd MARCH 2002

A Danny Dichio header in the second half of the game against Wimbledon saw Albion bounce back from a midweek defeat at Preston North End where they both missed a penalty and lost Jason Roberts for the rest of the season with a broken foot, leaving Dichio, Bob Taylor and Scott Dobie as the club's only fit strikers. Dichio's goal began a run to the end of the campaign where the Throstles racked up 26 points out of 30 to snatch second place from Wolverhampton Wanderers.

SATURDAY 3RD MARCH 1894

Joe Reader, Albion's goalkeeper, made his only appearance between the sticks for England. He was beaten twice as England drew 2-2 with Ireland in the quaintly named Solitude, Belfast.

SATURDAY 3RD MARCH 1951

Albion earned a valuable 1-1 draw at Liverpool's Anfield thanks to Andy McCall's first goal for the club having made his debut on January 20th of the same year, against Chelsea. McCall scored just two more goals for the Baggies before moving on to join Leeds United for £2,000 in August 1952.

SATURDAY 4TH MARCH 1950

Albion's record league crowd of 60,945 packed The Hawthorns to see Ronnie Allen's goalscoring debut in the 1-1 draw with Wolves.

SATURDAY 4TH MARCH 1967

The Baggies chucked away a 2-0 lead to lose the first League Cup final to be held at Wembley, beaten 3-2 in the end by Third Division QPR. Clive Clark scored Albion's goals against his old club, creating a competition record by scoring in every round and every game, totalling eight goals for the season. The defeat was one of the biggest shocks in cup history for not only were there two divisions between the sides, there were two goals at the break. Stories differ as to what happened at half-time, some versions suggesting manager Jimmy Hagan tore into his team, accusing them of taking the game too easily, while others say that he simply told them to carry on in the same manner. Either way, Rangers at least were a different side after the break and with the aid of what might best be described as "helpful" refereeing, they turned the game completely on its head.

SATURDAY 4TH MARCH 2000

Brian Little's final game in charge of Albion saw them trounced 3-0 at home by Birmingham City in an early kick-off. Little's despondent post-match comments were widely interpreted as saying, "I've had enough, get me out of here", and chairman Paul Thompson obliged two days later by relieving him of his duties at The Hawthorns.

SATURDAY 5TH MARCH 1898

Winger Benjamin Garfield made his solitary appearance for England, against Ireland in a 3-2 win in Belfast. He was accompanied in the England side by Albion full-back Billy Williams.

SATURDAY 5TH MARCH 1949

Albion suffered a 2-1 defeat at The Hawthorns to the eventual Division Two champions, Fulham. The defeat had a positive outcome, spurring the Throstles on to a sequence of eight games without defeat, which proved the springboard to eventual promotion to Division One. Billy Elliott got the Albion goal in front of 27,595 paying punters.

MONDAY 6TH MARCH 1905

Mr. H. Keys is re-elected as chairman following an EGM where the existing board resigns. Billy Bassett becomes a director on the newly constituted board and he and his colleagues set about the task of tackling the huge financial problems facing Albion, the club on the verge of extinction. In April of 1905, they launched the 'Shilling Fund' to raise money, in conjunction with the local newspapers the *Birmingham Evening Despatch* and *Sports Argus* and brewers Mitchells & Butlers.

SATURDAY 6TH MARCH 1937

The Hawthorns hosted its biggest-ever crowd, 64,815, for the 3-1 win over Arsenal in the sixth round of the FA Cup. Mahon scored twice and W. G. Richardson added the other in a game famous for a wonderful performance by Teddy Sandford at centre-half as the Baggies derailed any hopes Arsenal might have had of doing the league and cup double. They also ended up third before going on to win the title for the fourth time in six seasons in 1937/38. The game brought in receipts of £3,914. At modern-day prices, a similar crowd would bring in somewhere in the region of £2 million, and attract considerably more interest from Her Majesty's revenue collectors.

SUNDAY 6TH MARCH 1977

Winger Laurie Cunningham joined the Throstles from Orient in a £110,000 transfer, Johnny Giles signing the first component of the legendary 'Three Degrees'.

SATURDAY 7th MARCH 1959

Any lingering hopes of mounting a late title challenge were buried at Upton Park as Albion's late winter slump continued with a 3-1 defeat against the Hammers, Bobby Robson scoring for the Throstles. This was part of a sequence of seven games without a win that saw the Baggies finally end up in fifth place in the table, just a single point behind third-placed Arsenal, but 12 away from top spot.

SATURDAY 7th MARCH 1970

In spite of scoring the first goal of the game just a few minutes from the start, Albion slipped to a 2-1 defeat to Manchester City in the League Cup final at Wembley, going down in extra time on a bog-like pitch devastated by heavy snow in the week leading up to the game. Jeff Astle scored Albion's goal, becoming the first man to score in both an FA Cup and League Cup final at Wembley. Future Albion goalkeeping coach Joe Corrigan was outjumped by Astle for the goal.

WEDNESDAY 7th MARCH 1979

In the first leg of their Uefa Cup quarter-final, Albion were beaten 1-0 by Red Star Belgrade in front of an astonishing crowd of 95,300 in the former Yugoslavian capital.

SATURDAY 8th MARCH 1958

Albion hosted Manchester United in a Division One game just after the Munich disaster and won 4-0 in front of a huge crowd of 63,278, the second largest in Hawthorns history. Two goals from Ronnie Allen, another from Derek Kevan and an Ian Greaves own goal saw Albion to a comfortable win.

TUESDAY 8th MARCH 1977

Two goals from David Cross saw Albion clinch a rare win at Highbury, beating Arsenal 2-1. The crowd was a paltry 19,517.

FRIDAY 8th MARCH 1996

Albion signed Dutch master Richard Sneekes from Bolton Wanderers for £400,000 as Alan Buckley's team were battling relegation from Division One. Sneekes scored 10 goals in 13 games to drag the Throstles to mid-table safety.

SATURDAY 9TH MARCH 1963

Derek Kevan played his last game for the Albion, signing off with a hat-trick in a 6-1 win over Ipswich Town at The Hawthorns. He was then sold to Chelsea. Kevan admitted later that he had never felt at home with the training methods of managers Archie Macaulay and Gordon Clark, the two men who had tried to replace his mentor, Vic Buckingham.

WEDNESDAY 9TH MARCH 1966

Albion were beaten 2-1 at Upton Park in the first leg of the League Cup final, played as it was in those days, over two legs, Jeff Astle scoring for Albion. There was some dispute over West Ham's second goal, but it mattered little as the Throstles overturned the position to win the cup at The Hawthorns.

THURSDAY 9TH MARCH 2000

Gary Megson was appointed as Albion's new manager in succession to Brian Little, beginning a reign which lasted 222 matches. Frank Burrows was appointed as his assistant manager. His first job was to stave off relegation from Division One, a task achieved on the final day of the season.

SUNDAY 9TH MARCH 2008

Albion won a sixth round FA Cup tie at Bristol Rovers, impressing the millions watching the game on the BBC with a 5-1 win. Ishmael Miller scored a hat-trick to see off the challenge of the west country side, ensuring that the Baggies would be back at the new Wembley Stadium for the FA Cup semi-final.

SATURDAY 10TH MARCH 1956

After signing for the Baggies from Fulham, Bobby Robson made an inauspicious start to life at The Hawthorns as his debut saw Albion thumped 4-0 by Manchester City, 32,680 seeing the future knight's debut.

MONDAY 10TH MARCH 1969

Albion enjoyed a very rare win at Sunderland's Roker Park, Tony Brown getting the only goal of the game. Len Cantello made his debut for the Baggies.

SATURDAY 11TH MARCH 1911

Leicester Fosse – later Leicester City – were no match for the Baggies who went on their travels and returned home with two points in tow after a 3-2 victory in the East Midlands, Sid Bowser scoring twice, Harry Wright scoring too as Albion headed for the Second Division title.

SATURDAY 11TH MARCH 1972

After a £100,000 move across the Midlands from Leicester City, Ally Brown scored on his debut for the Throstles in a 1-1 draw with Crystal Palace at The Hawthorns.

SATURDAY 11TH MARCH 2000

The 'ginger ninja' Lee Hughes' strike gave the similarly carrot-topped Gary Megson a winning start to his managerial career as Albion beat Stockport County 1-0. But the victory was marred by a serious injury to Larus Sigurdsson, sidelined for nine months by a cruciate ligament injury, a particular blow as Sigurdsson had been among Albion's most consistent performers in a grim season.

SATURDAY 12TH MARCH 1977

Johnny Giles gave Albion debuts to Laurie Cunningham and Tony Godden, the pair getting off to a winning start as the Baggies beat Tottenham Hotspur 2-0 at White Hart Lane with goals from Bryan Robson and David Cross.

SATURDAY 13TH MARCH 1937

One of Albion's all-time greats, Len Millard, joined the club as an amateur. Millard ultimately went on to captain the club to the 1954 FA Cup win, enjoying a playing career with the Throstles that endured until his departure in 1958.

SATURDAY 13TH MARCH 1948

Striker Jack Haines scored on his Albion debut at West Ham United in a 2-0 win, Billy Elliott grabbing the other goal for the Baggies. Haines had a brief but prolific spell with the Throstles, scoring 23 times in 62 games and becoming a central figure as the team dashed towards promotion in the 1948/49 season, winning an England cap into the bargain, scoring on debut for his country against Switzerland.

SATURDAY 14TH MARCH 1931

A long range cross from skipper Tommy Glidden from just inside the opposition half was caught by a gust of wind and flummoxed the Everton goalkeeper who let it over his head to give Albion a win by the only goal in the FA Cup semi-final at Old Trafford. A massive crowd of 69,241 made it difficult for the Albion party to get into the ground before the game but at full time, they were celebrating the prospect of a first-ever appearance at Wembley, just eight years after the 'White Horse' cup final had made the place an instant legend and a Mecca for all footballers.

SATURDAY 15TH MARCH 1890

Charlie Perry won his first England cap, featuring against Ireland at the Ulster Cricket Ground in Belfast in a Home International game. Fellow Albion man Bob Roberts was in goal and didn't have a great deal to do as England won 9-1. Perry had to wait a further 12 months for a second cap, despite the win. England also won that one, 6-1 against Ireland at Molineux but it was a further two years before Perry played his third and final international, a 6-0 win over Wales at Stoke. Three caps, three wins, 21 goals for, two against. Perhaps he should have played more often.

SATURDAY 15TH MARCH 1947

Belfast boy Jack Vernon played his first senior game for the Throstles, the great centre-half featuring in a 3-2 defeat to West Ham United at Upton Park, Hodgetts and Elliott scoring for Albion. Vernon went on to become known as one of the very best centre-halves of his generation, and perhaps the very best footballing centre-half the Albion have ever employed.

SATURDAY 15TH MARCH 1997

Len Millard passed away at the age of 78. Millard captained the club and made a total of 627 appearances, scoring 18 goals. His greatest achievement was to lead the side up Wembley's 39 steps to collect the FA Cup from the Queen Mother in 1954 after he had kept the great Tom Finney quiet as the Throstles beat Preston North End 3-2 to win the final.

MONDAY 16TH MARCH 1914

Albion captain Bob McNeal made his England debut in a 2-0 win over Wales at Ninian Park, Cardiff. He also played in England's next game on April 4th 1914, a 3-1 defeat against Scotland at Hampden Park.

WEDNESDAY 16TH MARCH 1977

Having been thumped 7-0 at Portman Road earlier in the season, the Throstles exacted a modicum of revenge from Ipswich Town by beating them 4-0 under floodlights at The Hawthorns. Bryan Robson scored a hat-trick and Laurie Cunningham marked his home debut by scoring too as former Albion man Bobby Robson saw his Ipswich side played off the park.

SATURDAY 16TH MARCH 2002

'The Battle of Bramall Lane' took place at Sheffield United as promotion-chasing Albion carved the home side apart. A ragged United outfit had three men sent off, two of them, Santos and Suffo, dismissed within minutes of coming on as substitutes. After using all of their subs, two United men then mysteriously left the field injured, reducing the team to only six players. The referee Eddie Wolstenholme had no choice but to abandon the game with eight minutes left, and Albion 3-0 up, Scott Dobie scoring two and Derek McInnes adding the goal of the season, a ferocious first time drive from the edge of the box. Manager Gary Megson insisted afterwards Albion would not return to play again if the fixture had to be replayed but the authorities ultimately allowed the 3-0 scoreline to stand.

SATURDAY 17TH MARCH 1945

Albion beat Northampton Town 6-0 in a qualifying round of the wartime cup at The Hawthorns in front of 6,938. Ike Clarke registered a hat-trick, Heaselgrave, Johnson and an own goal completed the scoring.

SATURDAY 17TH MARCH 1951

Albion fell to a 5-0 defeat at Tottenham Hotspur's White Hart Lane. March 17th proved to be a very black day for the Baggies in the 1950s as it also saw them lose 5-0 away at Chelsea in 1954 and 4-0 at Bolton Wanderers in 1956.

MONDAY 18TH MARCH 1907

Jesse Pennington made his England debut at left full-back in a 1-1 draw with Wales at Fulham's Craven Cottage, beginning his legendary defensive partnership with Bob Crompton. Pennington went on to make 25 appearances in total for England, and would surely have had more had his career not been interrupted by the Great War. Nonetheless, in an era where England rarely played more than five games in a season, 25 caps was a very healthy haul for any player.

SATURDAY 18TH MARCH 1933

Albion humbled Portsmouth 4-2 at The Hawthorns with W. G. Richardson and Teddy Sandford both notching two goals. A crowd of 16,356 was in attendance.

SATURDAY 19TH MARCH 1887

Bob Roberts made his England debut in goal against Scotland at Leamington Road, Blackburn. He found himself on the losing side as England were beaten 3-2 by Scotland, but Roberts at least had the distinction of becoming Albion's first ever international footballer.

SATURDAY 19TH MARCH 1892

The Throstles won the FA Cup for the second time, beating Aston Villa in comprehensive fashion by three goals to nil at the Kennington Oval. The goals came from Geddes, Nicholls and Reynolds, who was later to play for Villa against Albion in the 1895 FA Cup final. It was a particularly sweet win given that Villa had been somewhat over confident in the days leading up to the game.

SATURDAY 19TH MARCH 1960

Albion recovered from being 2-0 down to Everton inside 12 minutes to win 6-2 at The Hawthorns, thanks largely to Derek 'The Tank' Kevan who scored five goals. David Burnside scored the other.

SATURDAY 19TH MARCH 2005

A 4-1 win at Charlton Athletic – Robert Earnshaw scored a hat-trick – set Albion up for a strong run in to the end of the season, enabling them to complete the 'Great Escape' from relegation on the final day.

SATURDAY 20TH MARCH 1954

Albion bounced back from a 5-0 defeat at Chelsea to beat Blackpool 2-1 at The Hawthorns to keep their chase for the league and cup double on course, a week ahead of their FA Cup semi-final meeting with Port Vale.

SATURDAY 20TH MARCH 1976

Goals from Joe Mayo and John Wile proved enough to beat Bolton Wanderers 2-0 at The Hawthorns in a game that was to prove pivotal to the season. With Albion hunting down those sides in the promotion spots, it looked as if Bolton would beat them to a place in the top flight, but this victory gave the Throstles fresh momentum and set them off on a run-in that included six wins, two draws and just one defeat as they pipped Bolton to third place by a single point.

WEDNESDAY 21ST MARCH 1979

A fortunate late goal for Red Star Belgrade gave them a 2-1 aggregate win over Albion in the Uefa Cup quarter-final, Cyrille Regis having levelled the aggregate scores by putting his side in front on the night earlier in the game.

SATURDAY 22ND MARCH 1890

For the second consecutive season, Everton were Albion's final-day opponents in the league and again, they were beaten, this time by four goals to one at Stoney Lane, Evans scoring twice, Wilson once and Pearson also notching to top the scoring charts for the season with 17 goals.

SATURDAY 22ND MARCH 1947

Jack Vernon played his first game at The Hawthorns as the Throstles beat Sheffield Wednesday 2-1 thanks to goals from Ike Clarke and George Drury. The post-war boom in attendances continued with 35,448 attending the game.

FRIDAY 22ND MARCH 2002

A late poacher's goal from Bob Taylor saw Albion edge to a 1-0 win in a Friday night televised game at Nottingham Forest, maintaining the pressure on Wolves in the chase for promotion.

WEDNESDAY 23RD MARCH 1966

Albion won the Football League Cup for the first and, so far, only time by beating West Ham United 4-1 at The Hawthorns in the second leg of the final, wiping off the first leg deficit of 2-1. In an awesome first-half performance, the Hammers, including soon-to-be World Cup winners Bobby Moore, Martin Peters and Geoff Hurst in their side, were swept aside by the Throstles. Goals from John Kaye, Tony Brown, Clive Clark and Graham Williams secured the cup in the first season in which Albion had entered the competition. Tony Brown scored in every round.

SATURDAY 23RD MARCH 1929

Jimmy Cookson was in the right place at the right time to score the only goal of the local derby between Black Country rivals Albion and Wolverhampton Wanderers, as the majority of the 24,340 crowd at Molineux were once again made to realise that they'd picked the wrong team to support!

SATURDAY 23RD MARCH 1907

Everton denied Albion another FA Cup final when they defeated the Throstles at the semi-final stage, beating them 2-1 in a game played at Bolton, hardly neutral territory. It was the second season in a row that Everton had beaten Albion in the cup, having won on home turf in the third round the year before.

SATURDAY 24TH MARCH 1888

The FA Cup came to West Bromwich for the first time as underdogs Albion defeated Preston North End 2-1 in the final at the Kennington Oval in front of 18,904 spectators. So sure were they of victory, Preston are alleged to have asked to be pictured with the cup before the game, to which the referee replied, "Don't you think you should win it first?" Jem Bayliss and George 'Spry' Woodhall got the goals that won the cup for a team made up of eleven Black Countrymen, a sharp contrast to the expensively assembled Preston side that had been recruited from across England and Scotland and would go on to become the legendary 'Invincibles' just twelve months later by winning the league and cup double.

MONDAY 24TH MARCH 1934

There were plenty of goals when Albion took on Sunderland at The Hawthorns, the Baggies ending a run of four defeats by beating the Rokermen 6-5, the goals being well shared around the team. Skipper Tommy Glidden scored twice against his fellow north-easterners, while Teddy Sandford, Joe Carter, W. G. Richardson and Wally Boyes also got a goal each. A mere 11,889 were in the ground to see the goalfest.

SATURDAY 25TH MARCH 2000

As part of the fight for survival, Gary Megson gave debuts to four players at Manchester City; Georges Santos, Neil Clement, Tony Butler and the returning Bob Taylor. The Baggies slipped to a 2-1 defeat at Maine Road but those four and Des Lyttle, the 'famous five' signed by Megson just prior to the transfer deadline, all played key parts in staving off relegation.

SATURDAY 26TH MARCH 1927

Albion completed a thumping 4-2 win over Newcastle United with goals from Jack Byers, Stan Davies, Joe Carter and a John Short penalty doing the trick. Despite the result, Albion finished bottom of the First Division. Newcastle ended up as champions.

SATURDAY 26TH MARCH 1949

Goals from Albion's strike force of Dave Walsh and Jack Haines were to prove vital as Albion bagged a draw with fellow promotion chasers Cardiff City at Ninian Park. The 2-2 scoreline prevented Cardiff stealing a march on the Throstles and Albion were able to steer clear of them over the season's final furlong to take the second promotion place behind Fulham.

SATURDAY 26TH MARCH 1988

In a virtual benefit for the Villa 'old boys', two goals from Andy Gray and another from Kenny Swain saw the Baggies to a 3-2 win over fellow strugglers Huddersfield Town as Ron Atkinson sought to reverse the damage inflicted on the season by Ron Saunders. After that win in Yorkshire, Albion won one and drew five of the last seven games to survive by a single point. Huddersfield took the drop with Reading and Sheffield United.

SATURDAY 27TH MARCH 1954

In a dramatic FA Cup semi-final at Villa Park, the Throstles finally overcame Port Vale of the Third Division to reach Wembley. Vale snatched the lead and looked as if they might hold on for a remarkable victory but a rare goal from Jimmy Dudley followed by a Ronnie Allen penalty against his old side took the Baggies to the twin towers for the third time. Allen said afterwards he had wondered if he should avoid taking the spot kick given his ties with Vale but said he would have felt too guilty if someone else had stepped up and missed. A crowd of 67,977 paid £20,086 for the privilege of being there.

TUESDAY 28TH MARCH 1893

Tom Perry won his only England cap, as Wales were defeated by three goals to nil at Wrexham. England's goals came from Smith and Wheldon with two. Albion's Billy Williams was also in the England team on the day.

SATURDAY 28TH MARCH 1914

Jesse Pennington enjoyed his benefit match in the end of season encounter with Sunderland which Albion won 2-1 thanks to a brace from Howard Gregory. A crowd of 23,366 paid tribute to the great full-back.

SUNDAY 29TH MARCH 1959

Legendary Albion goalscorer W. G. Richardson passed away, while playing in a charity game at Sheldon against a TV All-Star XI. He received a pass from Billy Elliott, turned the ball onwards, then 'fell and didn't get up'. He was picked up by Elliott and Harry Parkes, but he was already dead. He was just 49 and was still a member of the Albion coaching staff.

SATURDAY 29TH MARCH 1969

Walsall-born Allan Clarke, an Albion fan as a youngster, scored a late goal for Leicester City to defeat the Baggies in the FA Cup semi-final, played at Hillsborough in front of 52,207 fans. Leicester lost the final to Manchester City and were relegated from the top flight, which proves there is some kind of cosmic justice after all.

SATURDAY 29TH MARCH 2008

Albion completed a dramatic turnaround to come from 2-0 behind after 17 minutes and 3-2 down as the game entered injury time to defeat lowly Colchester United 4-3 and keep their hold on the promotion places. Two goals in three minutes from Kevin Phillips and Chris Brunt had brought Albion level just before the break, then James Morrison and Roman Bednar both struck goals in time added on to win a game that was seemingly lost.

SATURDAY 30TH MARCH 1912

Albion's FA Cup semi-final with Blackburn Rovers at Anfield ended up in a 0-0 stalemate in a game of few chances where defences were dominant. Blackburn were heading for the double at his stage, leading the First Division and going on to win the title.

WEDNESDAY 31ST MARCH 1954

In a game at Sunderland's Roker Park, Albion were defeated 2-1, a result which had a serious impact on their title push. Goalkeeper Norman Heath was badly injured in a challenge during the game and not only missed the FA Cup final at the end of the season but never played the game again. Ray Barlow went in goal for Albion against the Rokerites after Heath was carried off.

TUESDAY 31ST MARCH 1964

Called up late for the game because of injuries, youngster Mickey Fudge scored a hat-trick for the Baggies, Graham Williams adding another as reigning champions Everton were beaten 4-2 at The Hawthorns. Injury blighted his progress at The Hawthorns and he was released by Alan Ashman in June 1967, moving on to Exeter City.

SATURDAY 31ST MARCH 1984

Goals by Steve Mackenzie and Cyrille Regis ensured that Albion maintained their good record against Manchester United at The Hawthorns, the 2-0 win ending a sequence of three straight victories, keeper Paul Barron keeping clean sheets in all of them. This was to prove an important victory by the end of the campaign when Albion survived in the top flight by just three points.

THE ALBION
On This Day

WEST BROMWICH
ALBION

APRIL

SATURDAY 1st APRIL 1899

Billy Bassett scored his 77th and last goal for the Baggies, getting on the scoresheet in a 2-0 win over Newcastle United at Stoney Lane. Arthur Smith scored the other goal, his only one for Albion.

SATURDAY 1st APRIL 1995

Albion's striker Johnnie Nicholls, one half of the 'terrible twins' alongside Ronnie Allen in the 1950s, died on his way home from The Hawthorns after watching the Baggies lose 3-1 to Middlesbrough. He was 64.

MONDAY 1st APRIL 2002

Perhaps the most decisive day in the chase for promotion to the Premier League. After Wolves were beaten in an early kick-off at home to Manchester City, clear leaders in Division One, the Throstles overcame Coventry City by a single goal at Highfield Road, Bob Taylor scoring the crucial goal early on, the Baggies surviving the latter stages with just ten men after substitute Trevor Benjamin was dismissed for a somewhat boisterous challenge. Albion edged ahead of Wolves into second place in the table and had their fate in their own hands at last with just three games to go. Celebrating Manchester City friends had regaled Molineux with a chorus of "We're going up with the Albion". How right they were.

SATURDAY 2nd APRIL 1887

For the second successive season, Albion were beaten in the FA Cup final, this time by local rivals Aston Villa who came out on top 2-0 in the game played at The Oval. The omens pointed to defeat for Albion because the throstle, kept by the club at their headquarters at the Plough & Harrow pub, fell off its perch just before kick-off. This was an ex throstle, it had ceased to be.

SATURDAY 2nd APRIL 1892

John 'Baldy' Reynolds made his England debut in a 4-1 win over Scotland in Glasgow. Reynolds made a further seven appearances for his country, continuing as an international after leaving Albion for Aston Villa. Prior to playing for England, Reynolds had previously won five caps for Ireland while playing for Distillery.

SATURDAY 3RD APRIL 1886

The FA Cup final took place at The Oval, part of a big sporting day in the capital as the University Boat Race was also on. The cup final turned into a damp squib as Albion played out a goalless draw with Blackburn Rovers.

WEDNESDAY 3RD APRIL 1912

Blackburn Rovers were defeated in an FA Cup semi-final replay in Sheffield, Bob Pailor scoring the winning goal for the Baggies in extra time, the only goal in 210 minutes of football.

SATURDAY 3RD APRIL 1954

Having been ignored throughout a season where they couldn't stop scoring goals, Ronnie Allen and Johnnie Nicholls took to the field for England against Scotland at Hampden Park and both were on the scoresheet as England defeated the 'Auld Enemy' 4-2, Nicholls playing in his only game for England on his 23rd birthday. While those two were busy representing their country, a heavily depleted Albion side were beaten 1-0 by Wolves at The Hawthorns, effectively ending dreams of the league and cup double, sending the league title to Molineux. Nicholls played just once more for England – a 1-0 defeat against Yugoslavia in Belgrade – two months later.

SATURDAY 3RD APRIL 1993

Andy Hunt scored a hat-trick on his full league debut for the Throstles as Albion defeated Brighton & Hove Albion 3-1 and continued the chase for promotion under Ossie Ardiles.

MONDAY 4TH APRIL 1892

Albion posted a new league record by thumping Darwen 12-0. Pearson scored four, Bassett helped himself to a hat-trick, Reynolds scored twice and Nicholls, Geddes and an own goal completed the rout. Records show that only 1,109 were there to see the game, well down on the season average of 6,600.

THURSDAY 4TH APRIL 1963

Manager Archie Macaulay resigned after 18 months in the job, saying he had failed to settle in the area. His departure set off a string of behind-the-scenes changes at the club.

SATURDAY 5TH APRIL 1919

Thomas Patrick Magee, the only player to have won both the league and FA Cup with the Throstles, made his debut against Derby County in the Midland Victory League, the competition running in the aftermath of World War I prior to the resumption of the Football League. Magee, famously signed by the club while still a serving soldier, scored on debut, Cliff Sambrooke and Bob McNeal adding the others in a 3-1 win. Magee went on to make 434 appearances and score 18 goals for the club.

TUESDAY 6TH APRIL 1915

Freddie Reed made his league debut for the Baggies at The Hawthorns in a 3-2 win over Tottenham Hotspur. Reed went on to play more than 150 games for the first team, over 200 for the reserves and, upon his retirement as a player in 1927, he was appointed as trainer-coach, a position he held until 1950.

WEDNESDAY 7TH APRIL 1965

Legendary manager Bill Shankly suffered a rare defeat at Anfield as an imperious Albion defeated Liverpool 3-0 with goals from John Kaye, Clive Clark and Bobby Hope.

MONDAY 7TH APRIL 1969

A crowd of 24,173 were lucky to witness a real humdinger between Albion and Tottenham Hotspur, the Throstles eventually coming out on top in the seven-goal thriller, Jeff Astle scoring twice, Bobby Hope and Tony Brown getting the others in the 4-3 win.

MONDAY 7TH APRIL 1975

Following the departure of manager Don Howe as manager after being told that his contract would not be renewed at the end of the campaign, Brian Whitehouse took charge of things for the rest of the season as Albion's caretaker manager.

SATURDAY 7TH APRIL 1979

Martyn Bennett made his Albion debut, filling in at full-back, as Albion edged past Everton by a single Ally Brown goal in a tight encounter, keeping them in the title hunt.

THURSDAY 8TH APRIL 1937

Billy Bassett passed away at the age of 68, having been player, captain, director and chairman of the club during his long association with the Albion. His death on the eve of the FA Cup semi-final had a huge impact on the club and was possibly a contributory factor in the club's defeat.

SATURDAY 8TH APRIL 1978

The Baggies were beaten 3-1 by Ipswich Town in the FA Cup semi-final at Highbury, Tony Brown scoring a late penalty for Albion, but it was not enough to salvage a game lost early on as the Tractor Boys got into a 2-0 lead in the early exchanges. Mick Martin was sent off late in the game, while skipper John Wile played the bulk of the fixture swathed in bandages with blood pouring from a head wound sustained as he clashed heads with Brian Talbot in trying to prevent Ipswich's opening goal. Manager Ron Atkinson had earlier made the mistake of visiting Wembley accompanied by the BBC's *Football Focus* programme, an act of hubris that proved costly as Ipswich sat watching the broadcast before the game. Manager Bobby Robson said that he didn't need to give a team talk after watching that.

SATURDAY 9TH APRIL 1932

Both George 'Cocky' Shaw and Harold Pearson played their one and only game for England in the end of season 3-0 win over Scotland at Wembley Stadium.

SATURDAY 9TH APRIL 1949

Defender Joe Kennedy made his Albion debut as a Morrow goal gave the Throstles a 1-0 victory at Luton Town's Kenilworth Road. He went on to play another 396 games in the stripes as one of Albion's finest ever defenders, picking up an FA Cup winner's medal along the way in 1954.

TUESDAY 9TH APRIL 1963

Following Archie Macaulay's departure as manager five days earlier, Major H. Wilson Keys also decided to step down as chairman of the club, a position he had held since 1948. He remained on the board as a director.

SATURDAY 10TH APRIL 1886

Albion were defeated by Blackburn Rovers at Derby County in the FA Cup Final replay, Blackburn scoring twice without reply. A crowd of 16,144 were there to see it. It was Albion's first FA Cup final, coming at only the third attempt as they established their credentials as a cup fighting side.

SATURDAY 10TH APRIL 1920

Albion clinched their first, and so far only, league title by beating Bradford City 3-1 at The Hawthorns. A crowd of 29,500 saw goals from Jephcott, Bentley and Bowser create history, the Baggies topping the pile with four games still to play. They ended the season on 60 points and scored 104 goals. While the celebrations were going on in the Black Country, Jesse Pennington made his 25th and last England appearance in a 5-4 victory over Scotland at Hillsborough. He played just once more for his country.

SATURDAY 10TH APRIL 1937

Clearly affected by the death of Billy Bassett just two days earlier, a substantially below par Albion were well beaten 4-1 by Preston North End in the FA Cup semi-final at Highbury, Walter Robbins getting Albion's consolation goal. Teddy Sandford said later that following the minute's silence before the game, "I was tearful for most of the first half". On the day of Bassett's funeral, 100,000 mourners lined the streets of West Bromwich.

WEDNESDAY 10TH APRIL 1963

Jimmy Hagan was appointed manager in succession to Archie Macaulay, beginning a controversial four-year reign at The Hawthorns that brought Albion the League Cup in 1966, as well as defeat in the 1967 Final. Hagan signed many of the 1968 FA Cup-winning side including Jeff Astle, and was responsible for the elevation of Tony Brown into the first team.

WEDNESDAY 11TH APRIL 1973

Jeff Astle made his 350th appearance for the Albion, scoring in the 4-1 home win over Everton, Asa Hartford and a brace from David Shaw completing the rout.

SATURDAY 12TH APRIL 1924

A poor crowd of just 8,003, the lowest of the season, saw Albion take Notts County to pieces, winning 5-0 with goals from George James and 'Tug' Wilson, who both scored twice, and Ivor Jones.

WEDNESDAY 12TH APRIL 1978

Albion bounced back from the disappointment of FA Cup semi-final defeat against Ipswich just a few days earlier to maintain their push for a Uefa Cup slot, goals from Cyrille Regis and Paddy Mulligan, his first for the club, defeating Newcastle United at The Hawthorns.

SATURDAY 13TH APRIL 1889

Billy Bassett made his England debut and marked it by scoring two goals in two minutes. Despite his brace, he still ended up on the losing side as Scotland beat England 3-2. In the course of an exceptional England career in days when international fixtures were few and far between, Bassett won 16 caps and scored seven goals.

SATURDAY 13TH APRIL 1912

Freddie Morris scored on his Albion debut, notching the only goal of the game as the Baggies beat Sunderland at The Hawthorns. The Tipton-born forward went on to become one of only 12 men to score more than 100 goals for Albion.

THURSDAY 13TH APRIL 1961

Tony Brown signed for the Throstles as an apprentice, thereby beginning the greatest playing career in the history of the Albion.

SATURDAY 13TH APRIL 2002

On one of the most emotional afternoons in the club's history... An injury-time penalty from full-back Igor Balis gave Albion a 1-0 win at Bradford City, Bob Taylor having been fouled in the penalty area as the game looked to be petering out into a draw. That result meant that Albion went into their final game of the season, at home to Crystal Palace, knowing that a win would take them into the Premier League for the first time.

TUESDAY 14th APRIL 1903

Ted 'Cock' Pheasant enjoyed his benefit game against Wolves, a fixture also notable for Jesse Pennington wearing the Albion shirt for the first time, though he was to wait another six months before making his full debut.

THURSDAY 14th APRIL 1968

At the third attempt, Albion finally edged past Liverpool in the sixth round of the FA Cup, winning the second replay at Manchester City's Maine Road in extra time. Goals from Jeff Astle and Clive Clark proved crucial in a thrilling cup-tie in front of a crowd of 56,139, earning £18,419 in gate receipts.

SATURDAY 14th APRIL 1973

John Wile played his 100th league game for the Throstles, featuring in the 1-0 defeat to Liverpool at Anfield.

SATURDAY 15th APRIL 1972

Albion won at Molineux, Tony Brown scoring the only goal of the game to beat Wolves in front of a 30,619 crowd.

SATURDAY 15th APRIL 1978

The Baggies continued their strong end-of-season form with a 3-1 win at Manchester City to stay in the running for a place in Europe. Cyrille Regis helped himself to a stunning goal, Laurie Cunningham and Ally Brown also chipping in as Malcolm Allison's City crumbled.

SATURDAY 15th APRIL 2000

For a side that was looking to dig itself out of relegation trouble, the Baggies certainly seemed to have a death wish, ending up taking just a point from a game against Bolton Wanderers which they'd led on three occasions. Richard Sneekes' penalty made it 1-0, then after the visitors drew level, Sean Flynn gave Albion a half-time lead. The Throstles slipped behind in the second half but Bob Taylor equalised against his old club after 79 minutes and when Adam Oliver made it 4-3 with two minutes left, the points looked safe, only for Bergsson to score an injury time equaliser that left Albion in deep trouble.

MONDAY 16TH APRIL 1900

The end of an era as Albion played their final game at the Stoney Lane ground in front of 5,187 spectators. Albion celebrated by crushing Nottingham Forest 8-0 with a hat-trick from Billy Walker, two apiece for Dick Roberts and 'Chippy' Simmons, and another from Jack Chadburn. Thereafter, Albion played their home games at The Hawthorns.

FRIDAY 16TH APRIL 1965

Not such a Good Friday as the Baggies were crushed 6-1 at West Ham United, the Hammers' striker Brian Dear knocking in five goals for the Londoners inside 20 minutes. Jeff Astle got the slight consolation of another goal for Albion, the tenth of his first season in the stripes.

SATURDAY 17TH APRIL 1971

Amid extraordinary scenes at Elland Road, Albion recorded their first away win of the season to beat Leeds United 2-1. Following Albion's second goal from Jeff Astle – when Colin Suggett was ruled to be not interfering with play despite being offside – there was a pitch invasion from irate supporters, while Leeds boss Don Revie also confronted the referee. The defeat cost Leeds the title that went instead to Arsenal who won the double, and some say it cost Leeds the league the following year too. Elland Road was closed at the beginning of the following season too as punishment for the crowd trouble, Leeds dropping points as they had to play elsewhere.

SATURDAY 17TH APRIL 1976

A 2-0 win over Nottingham Forest at The Hawthorns set Albion up for promotion back to the top flight in Johnny Giles' first season in charge of the club. Mick Martin and Willie Johnston were the goalscorers against Brian Clough's team. 26,580 were in the ground to watch the Throstles in sparkling form.

TUESDAY 17TH APRIL 1979

A 1-0 defeat at Bristol City saw Albion's title challenge fatally falter, a flu epidemic and sheer exhaustion taking its toll on a thin squad as the Throstles played their third game in four days as they tackled the fixture backlog caused by the winter weather.

FRIDAY 18TH APRIL 1952

Jesse Carver was appointed as Albion's manager-coach. The progressive football thinker with extensive coaching experience in Italy went on to do much of the groundwork ahead of the 'Team of the Century' season of 1953/54.

MONDAY 18TH APRIL 1960

Birmingham City were taken apart at St. Andrew's by a rampant Albion side who celebrated Good Friday with a 7-1 win. Both Derek Kevan and Ronnie Allen scored hat-tricks while Alec Jackson also grabbed a goal. To add injury to insult, goalkeeper Jock Wallace kicked a clearance into the crowd and knocked out a young supporter. Birmingham had a measure of revenge by drawing 1-1 at The Hawthorns the following day.

SUNDAY 18TH APRIL 2004

Jason Koumas scored a late goal to defeat Sunderland 1-0 at the Stadium of Light to virtually secure an immediate return to the Premier League. The Black Cats were Albion's closest rivals for the second automatic promotion spot and placed their visitors under intense pressure throughout the game but in a classic '1-0 to the Albion' afternoon, the Baggies were tight at the back and pinched the game through a Lloyd Dyer-inspired breakaway.

SATURDAY 19TH APRIL 1958

Albion provided England with two players, Derek Kevan and Don Howe, as they smashed Scotland 4-0 at Hampden Park in the Home International Championship, prior to heading off for the 1958 World Cup finals. Kevan scored twice, Bobby Charlton and Bryan Douglas added the other goals.

SATURDAY 19TH APRIL 1969

The Baggies completed an emphatic week in the First Division; four games played, all four won. Having won 1-0 at Molineux, they proceeded to reel off a trio of victories at The Hawthorns, beating West Ham United 3-1 and Manchester City 2-0 before rounding it off with a 5-1 hammering of Newcastle United – John Kaye, Asa Hartford, Tony Brown, Clive Clark and Jeff Astle were all on target. Albion played nine games in the first 23 days of April.

SATURDAY 20TH APRIL 1895

Albion were beaten in their fifth FA Cup final by local rivals Aston Villa who had also defeated the Throstles in the 1889 final. Villa scored the only goal of the game after just 39 seconds in front of a crowd of 42,652 at the first final held at Crystal Palace, the crowd paying receipts of £1,545.

SATURDAY 20TH APRIL 1912

The Baggies and Second Division Barnsley played out a very dour FA Cup Final stalemate at Crystal Palace, the game ending as a goalless draw on an afternoon when both sides were so poor they were lucky to score nil. Cup final receipts of £3,768 were taken from a crowd of 55,213.

SATURDAY 21ST APRIL 1883

A first-ever trophy came the Albion's way after they beat Stoke City by three goals to two to lift the Staffordshire Cup in Stoke, Timmins, Bunn and Bell scoring the crucial goals.

MONDAY 21ST APRIL 1930

Tottenham Hotspur were beaten 4-3 at The Hawthorns, one of a sequence of seven straight league wins that heralded the emergence of the team that would go on to win the FA Cup and promotion double the following year, extending the winning sequence to 11.

SATURDAY 21ST APRIL 1973

A 1-0 home defeat to Norwich City all but condemned the Throstles to relegation from the top flight for the first time in a quarter of a century.

SUNDAY 21ST APRIL 2002

A 2-0 win over Crystal Palace clinched a place in the Premier League for the first time, Albion beating Wolves to automatic promotion. Goals from Darren Moore and Bob Taylor, along with a superb early save from Russell Hoult got the job done, the crowd pouring onto the pitch after the final whistle before they were eventually cleared to allow the staff and players to go on a lap of honour.

MONDAY 22ND APRIL 1895

In the final game of the season, Albion were required to beat Sheffield Wednesday by five clear goals to avoid playing in the 'Test matches' to avoid relegation – an early version of the play-offs. A Stoney Lane crowd of 8,217 saw Albion do the job with a goal to spare, Jasper Geddes (2), Tom Green, Tom Hutchinson, Tom Perry and Roddy McLeod getting on the scoresheet in the 6-0 victory.

MONDAY 22ND APRIL 1935

In a dress rehearsal for the FA Cup Final five days later, Albion and Sheffield Wednesday played out a 1-1 draw at The Hawthorns. The Baggies played a weakened side, and made no fewer than five changes for Wembley with Bill Richardson, Tommy Glidden, Joe Carter, Jimmy Edwards and Teddy Sandford all returning to the colours on the big day.

WEDNESDAY 22ND APRIL 1964

Following a long-running rift with Jimmy Hagan that dated back to the 'tracksuit revolt' of the previous December, full-back Don Howe finally left Albion to join Arsenal for a then record fee of £45,000. That paved the way for Howe to become a coach at Highbury, the mastermind behind their 1970/71 league and cup double season.

FRIDAY 22ND APRIL 1966

In a gesture of extreme generosity, Leicester City defender John Sjoberg scored two own goals to help the Baggies on their way to a 5-1 win over the Foxes at The Hawthorns. More conventional goals came from Jeff Astle and a brace from John Kaye.

SATURDAY 22ND APRIL 2006

A genuinely dreadful performance at Newcastle United saw Albion tumble to a 3-0 defeat and thereby slump to relegation from the Premier League under Bryan Robson. The only positive note was that the scoreline wasn't worse.

SATURDAY 23RD APRIL 1932

Joe Carter and W. G. Richardson scored in a 2-0 win over Chelsea at Stamford Bridge, Walter Robbins making his Albion debut in the fixture.

MONDAY 24TH APRIL 1899

Albion were thrashed 7-1 at local rivals Aston Villa in the final game of the season as Villa clinched the league title ahead of Liverpool. It was also the final game for Billy Bassett, who brought down the curtain on his Albion career, as a player at least. He later returned to serve as a director, and then chairman, of the club.

WEDNESDAY 24TH APRIL 1912

Barnsley defeated Albion 1-0 in extra time in the FA Cup final replay at Bramall Lane, Sheffield in another lacklustre affair dominated by the Tykes' defensive tactics. The location of the 'neutral' ground in Barnsley's home county was the subject of some controversy.

SATURDAY 24TH APRIL 1976

A ferocious volley from Tony Brown saw Albion beat Oldham Athletic 1-0 at Boundary Park, thereby clinching promotion back to the top flight in the first season under player-manager Johnny Giles. It capped a strong second half of the campaign which saw the Throstles surge up the league table after a troublesome early season as the payers struggled to adapt to Giles' style of possession football.

SATURDAY 24TH APRIL 2004

Albion's promotion to the top flight was confirmed without them having to kick a ball as Sunderland failed to win their early kick-off game, the Baggies getting the news from the big screens at The Hawthorns as they warmed up for the fixture with relegated Bradford City, managed by former Albion player and future manager, Bryan Robson. Albion celebrated elevation to the Premier League by winning the game 2-0, Geoff Horsfield and Lee Hughes getting the goals.

SATURDAY 25TH APRIL 1931

The Throstles secured the first leg of their unique FA Cup and promotion double by defeating Birmingham City at Wembley Stadium to collect the trophy for the third time, the first time at the new national stadium in the capital. Two goals from W. G. Richardson saw off First Division Blues, the pre-match favourites, in front of a crowd of 90,368 supporters, 2-1 the final score.

THURSDAY 26TH APRIL 1900

The Staffordshire Cup was Albion's once again after they beat Burslem Port Vale 5-0 in a replayed final at Villa Park. Two goals each from Walker and Roberts, and another from Simmons, gave Albion revenge for defeat in the Birmingham Senior Cup by the same scoreline back on December 11th 1899. The first Staffordshire final was played on December 4th 1899, a 1-1 draw with Simmons scoring Albion's goal. The replay had been scheduled for February 26th 1900, but was postponed due to heavy rain.

SATURDAY 27TH APRIL 1935

Two late goals saw Albion go down to Wembley defeat for the first time as Sheffield Wednesday won the FA Cup by four goals to two. Wally Boyes and Ted Sandford were on the mark for the Baggies.

SATURDAY 27TH APRIL 1968

The Throstles booked a trip to Wembley to take part in the FA Cup final by beating Birmingham City 2-0 at Villa Park in a pulsating semi-final. Goalkeeper John Osborne was inspired as Birmingham missed a number of chances, while, at the other end, Jeff Astle and Tony Brown did not.

SATURDAY 27TH APRIL 1991

Albion drew 1-1 with Port Vale at The Hawthorns. Don Goodman got the goal but the Baggies also contrived to miss two penalties. This was the third of five successive 1-1 draws that rounded out the campaign. Had just one of them been won, Albion would not have been relegated.

MONDAY 28TH APRIL 1902

Having won both the Second Division and the reserves league, two Albion sides met in a challenge match in front of 807 spectators. The reserves won 2-1, Smith and Buck getting their goals after Dorsett had put the 'first team' ahead. At the end of the game, Mr. T. H. Sidney, the vice-president of the Football League congratulated skipper Dan Nurse on the teams' successes. The Second Division championship trophy was not presented as it was elsewhere, but the reserves took possession of the Birmingham League Championship Shield.

SATURDAY 28TH APRIL 1951

Frank Griffin made his Albion debut at Sunderland's Roker Park on the final day of the season. The Throstles fought out a 1-1 draw, coming home with a point thanks to a Ronnie Allen goal.

SATURDAY 28TH APRIL 1962

Albion signed off the 1961/62 season by hammering Blackpool 7-1, Derek Kevan scoring four, Don Howe, John 'Shack' Lovatt and Bobby Robson also contributing. It meant that Kevan had scored ten goals in the last five games of the season as the Baggies collected all ten points from those games. Prior to kick-off, Howe was presented with the Midland Footballer of the Year award by Albion's chairman, Major H. Wilson Keys.

SATURDAY 29TH APRIL 1911

The Throstles went into the final game of the season needing a point to secure promotion back to the top flight. They went one better, a Freddie Buck penalty making sure in a 1-0 win over Huddersfield Town at The Hawthorns in front of a crowd of 30,135. Tottenham won the divisional title.

MONDAY 29TH APRIL 1912

The season came to its conclusion with a 0-0 home draw against Oldham Athletic, bringing a halt to an exhausting sequence of 13 games inside 31 days, including two FA Cup semi-finals and two FA Cup finals.

MONDAY 29TH APRIL 1968

Albion won a remarkable game against Manchester United 6-3 at The Hawthorns, Jeff Astle scoring a hat-trick, Ronnie Rees, Tony Brown and Asa Hartford also weighing in with goals. Within a month, Albion would go on to win the FA Cup and United would be the Champions of Europe.

SATURDAY 30TH APRIL 1960

Bobby Hope became the youngest player ever to play for the Albion at The Hawthorns – five months before his 17th birthday – making his debut in a First Division game against Arsenal. Alec Jackson ended the season on a high with a goal as Albion beat the Gunners 1-0.

THE ALBION
On This Day

MAY

SATURDAY 1ST MAY 1920

The Throstles were presented with the league championship trophy at The Hawthorns after beating Chelsea 4-0 to conclude a record-breaking season as they became the first side to amass 60 points in the First Division. A crowd of 35,668 saw Albion hold the trophy for the last time until they collected it for winning the Football League Championship in 2008.

SATURDAY 1ST MAY 1954

Len Millard lifted the FA Cup as Albion won it for the fourth time by beating Preston North End at Wembley Stadium, 3-2. Two goals from Ronnie Allen, including a memorable penalty which goalkeeper Jimmy Sanders could not bear to watch from the other end, set up Frank Griffin to clinch the trophy with a late winner. Albion also finished second in the First Division, coming within a whisker of becoming the first team to do the league and FA Cup double in the 20th century.

WEDNESDAY 1ST MAY 1968

Jeff Astle scored a second hat-trick in successive games as Albion beat West Ham United 3-1 at The Hawthorns as their preparations for Wembley saw them hitting top goalscoring form.

SATURDAY 2ND MAY 1931

Only one team has ever won the FA Cup and promotion to the top flight in the same season – Albion. Already the cup holders, promotion was clinched at The Hawthorns with a 3-2 win over Charlton Athletic in front of a packed house of 52,415 supporters. Teddy Sandford, Tommy Glidden and W. G. Richardson got the goals.

SATURDAY 2ND MAY 1992

The ignominious Bobby Gould era came to an end as Albion beat Shrewsbury Town 3-1 at the Gay Meadow, with goals from Strodder, Shakespeare and Taylor. The mood was anything but cheery however, as Albion fans carried a coffin around Shrewsbury and into the ground to symbolise the club's demise over recent seasons. Gould was quickly axed as manager as Albion failed even to reach the play-offs in their first ever season in the Third Division.

DARTMOUTH PARK PRODUCED A FLORAL TRIBUTE TO THE FA CUP WINNERS AFTER THE TRIUMPH OVER PRESTON ON 1ST MAY 1954

SATURDAY 3rd MAY 1924

Albion ended the season in the grand manner by beating Sheffield United 3-1 at The Hawthorns, thanks largely to a Bobby Blood hat-trick, one of them coming from the penalty spot.

SATURDAY 3rd MAY 1930

Southampton were put to the sword with a final day 5-1 beating at The Hawthorns. Jimmy Cookson scored four of them to complete an astounding sequence of 11 goals in four matches, having scored four against Hull City on April 19th, one versus Spurs on April 21st and two against Stoke City on April 26th. Cookson ended the campaign with 33 league goals.

WEDNESDAY 3rd MAY 1967

Jimmy Hagan's tenure as manager came to its end in the wake of the League Cup final defeat to QPR a few weeks earlier, his abrasive, uncompromising manner ultimately proving his undoing after he regularly managed to fall out with players who took a dislike to his disciplinarian style. Nonetheless, Hagan was a very shrewd judge of players and he did a great deal of the groundwork in piecing together the side that went on to win the FA Cup twelve months later.

SATURDAY 4th MAY 1946

Albion embarked on an 'end of the war' tour that took in visits to Belgium and Luxembourg and defeated Fola Jeunesse at Esch-sur-Alzette, winning by five goals to one with strikes from Frank Hodgetts, Billy Elliott, Butler and two from Ike Clarke. The tour also saw them lose 5-4 to a Belgian XI and draw 1-1 at Anderlecht, Hodgetts scoring again.

SUNDAY 5th MAY 2008

The Throstles clinched the Championship title with a 2-0 win over QPR at Loftus Road, Kim Do-Heon and Chris Brunt scoring the goals that sealed the title in front of a travelling support mostly dressed as superheroes in tribute to 'Superkev', Kevin Phillips, who, it turned out, was playing his last game for the Albion. Brunt's late equaliser in the 1-1 draw at home to Southampton on April 29th had already made promotion all but mathematically certain.

SATURDAY 6TH MAY 1922

Jesse Pennington brought another era to an end as he played his final game for the Albion at the age of 38 years and 256 days. It was a painful farewell as he and his team were on the wrong end of a 4-1 scoreline against Liverpool at The Hawthorns. Pennington finished on 495 senior games for the club without ever scoring a goal. He won the league title with the Throstles but never got an FA Cup winner's medal; defeat in the 1912 final to Barnsley was the closest he came.

SATURDAY 6TH MAY 1944

In the second leg of the final, the Baggies beat Nottingham Forest 4-3 at the City Ground in front of 15,177 supporters to clinch the Midland Wartime Cup. It represented something of a surprise after the first leg had ended 2-2 at The Hawthorns.

MONDAY 6TH MAY 1957

Derek Kevan marked his England debut by scoring in their 2-1 win over Scotland at Wembley Stadium, Duncan Edwards registering the other England goal in front of a capacity crowd of 100,000. 'The Tank' went on to score eight goals in 14 games for his country, a scoring record of which to be rightly proud.

TUESDAY 7TH MAY 1901

Dan Nurse joined Albion from Wolverhampton Wanderers, the beginning of a remarkable career in the Black Country. Nurse was the Albion team captain and the driving inspiration behind the side that won Division Two in 1901/02, and later on he filled the disparate roles of supporter, shareholder, scout and director, before being elected a life member of the club in 1920.

SUNDAY 7TH MAY 2000

In a game they had to win to guarantee survival, playing against the already-crowned First Division champions Charlton Athletic, 'survival Sunday' saw the Baggies produce a powerful performance to win 2-0 with goals from long-term Albion heroes Richard Sneekes and 'Super' Bob Taylor, thus condemning Walsall to the drop as they lost at Ipswich Town.

FRIDAY 8th MAY 1992

In a move designed to blow away the miseries of the previous two seasons, Osvaldo Ardiles was appointed Albion manager in succession to Bobby Gould. The Argentine World Cup winner returned the club to its attacking, adventurous roots, ultimately leading the club to promotion by winning the Wembley play-off final the following May and beginning the long haul back to English football's top table.

SUNDAY 8th MAY 1994

In another end-of-season game that saw Albion staring down the barrel of relegation before kick-off, the Throstles earned the all-important victory that kept them in Division One. Lee Ashcroft scored the only goal of the game for Keith Burkinshaw's side at Portsmouth's Fratton Park, an estimated 10,000 Baggies swelling the crowd of 17,629.

SATURDAY 9th MAY 1925

The Lord Mayor of Birmingham's Charity Cup came back to the Black Country as Albion beat Birmingham in the final at St. Andrew's, George James scoring twice and Jack Byers adding the other to secure Albion's triumph over the Second City club.

TUESDAY 10th MAY 1960

Derek Kevan brought down the curtain on his England career by playing in the 8-0 victory over Mexico at Wembley, 'the Tank' surprisingly failing to get on the scoresheet, something of a rarity.

WEDNESDAY 10th MAY 1995

Albion went to Cheltenham Town to play a friendly in aid of the Pied Piper Fund Appeal and were beaten 3-2. Assistant boss Arthur Mann played his only game for the club, having played against us in the victorious Manchester City side that won the 1970 League Cup, ending up on the scoresheet along with Gary Strodder. After he left the Albion, Mann took up work in a local factory before tragically dying in a work-related accident – his shirt from that League Cup final still hangs in the East Stand at The Hawthorns. Ronnie Allen also made a cameo appearance in the game as a late substitute, his final game for the Throstles at the age of 66.

SATURDAY 11TH MAY 1929

Joe Carter registered a goal for England as he played his part in the comfortable 5-1 win over Belgium in Brussels, a rare overseas jaunt for the national side in the Roaring Twenties.

FRIDAY 11TH MAY 1979

The Baggies consolidated their hold on second place in the top flight by going to Villa Park and returning home with a 1-0 win, John Trewick notching the only goal of the game. A week later, needing only to avoid defeat to Nottingham Forest in the final game of the season to finish second in Division One for the first time in 25 years, a Trevor Francis goal demoted the Throstles to third.

MONDAY 11TH MAY 1981

In the first game of their three-match tour of North America, Cyrille Regis scored in a 2-1 defeat against Vancouver Whitecaps. Elsewhere on tour, they beat Portland Timbers on the 13th, Kevin Summerfield scoring the only goal of the game, while they completed a 2-1 win over Edmonton Drillers in their final fixture, Regis and Summerfield scoring.

SATURDAY 11TH MAY 1991

Another end-of-season thriller, but this one did not go Albion's way as perhaps the most depressing season in the club's history ended with the Baggies relegated to the third tier of the league for the first time ever. On the day, needing a win to have any hope of survival, they drew 1-1 with Bristol Rovers at Twerton Park, Bath, Kwame Ampadu scoring, but they still took the drop by two clear points. Leicester City survived instead.

SATURDAY 12TH MAY 1951

SC Wacker of Austria pitched up at The Hawthorns as part of the celebrations for the 'Festival of Britain'. In a seven-goal thriller, the visitors came away as the 4-3 winners in front of a crowd of 16,074, Ronnie Allen scoring twice, the great Ray Barlow also getting a goal. Two days later, Barlow and Arthur Smith scored in the 2-0 win over FC Floriana, the second of the 'Festival' games.

TUESDAY 13th MAY 1902

Albion secretary Frank Heaven resigned at a Board meeting, the minutes citing "a disagreement with the Board over Club policy". As de facto team manager too, a major change in the direction of the club was in the offing, the youthful Fred Everiss taking over the post as secretary-manager, one he held until the summer of 1948.

SATURDAY 13th MAY 1967

The Throstles ended the 1966/67 season in emphatic fashion by thumping Newcastle United 6-1 at The Hawthorns, Tony Brown netting a hat-trick, Kenny Foggo, Graham Williams and Clive Clark also scoring goals against the Geordies. It brought an end to a sequence of four straight wins, and seven out of eight, through to the end of the campaign, taking them well clear of any relegation concerns.

TUESDAY 13th MAY 2003

Bob Taylor enjoyed a well-deserved testimonial game at The Hawthorns as Albion beat a Bryan Robson All-Star XI in front of 16,017 supporters. Taylor, injured in his final senior game for Albion against Newcastle United two days earlier after having been recalled to the side, much to his surprise, after sitting out the bulk of the season, was forced to play much of the game in goal.

SATURDAY 14th MAY 1977

Johnny Giles played his final senior game at The Hawthorns prior to resigning his post as player-manager at the end of the season, for the second season running, though this time, there was sadly no talking him out of it. He enjoyed a winning finale at least, goals from Mick Martin, Laurie Cunningham and David Cross beating Stoke City 3-1.

SATURDAY 14th MAY 1983

One of Albion's greatest servants, John Wile, played his 500th and last league game for the club, fittingly enough at Roker Park where his career had begun with Sunderland, a 1-1 draw seeing him on his way, Garry Thompson scoring for Albion. In total, Wile made 619 appearances for the Throstles, only one of them as a substitute, scoring 29 goals.

TUESDAY 15TH MAY 1900

The Board of directors set in motion the sequence of events that was to take Albion away from Stoney Lane to their new permanent home at The Hawthorns. A Board meeting resolved that, "The lease for the ground at the corner of Halfords Lane and Birmingham Road be signed and sealed with the seal of the company". Over a century later, it remains one of the better ideas the club has ever had.

SATURDAY 15TH MAY 1920

League champions Albion won the Football Association's Charity Shield outright for the first and only time to date, beating FA Cup winners Tottenham Hotspur 2-0, Andy Smith scoring both goals in front of 38,168 spectators paying £2,828 in receipts.

WEDNESDAY 15TH MAY 1929

Joe Carter was on the mark for England again, knocking in a brace as England battled to a 4-3 win over Spain in Madrid as part of a brief European sojourn.

SUNDAY 15TH MAY 2005

Bryan Robson's team became the first Premier League side to escape relegation after being bottom of the table at Christmas. In a rollercoaster afternoon where results involving Crystal Palace, Norwich City and Southampton were every bit as important, Albion began the day bottom of the table and were still there at half-time. Second-half goals from Geoff Horsfield and Kieran Richardson saw off the visitors, Portsmouth, at The Hawthorns, while both Norwich and Southampton were well beaten. With ten minutes to go, Palace looked set to survive, but a late Charlton goal relegated them and reprieved the Throstles instead. Scenes of mass hysteria ensued at The Hawthorns after crowd and players had endured a nail-biting wait for the Palace result to be confirmed.

SATURDAY 16TH MAY 1970

The 'friendly' end-of-season Anglo-Italian tournament saw Albion's fixture at Lanerossi Vicenza abandoned after 76 minutes because of fighting between the players, the officials and the crowd, all the bases being covered. Allan Glover scored for Albion in the 1-1 draw.

WEDNESDAY 17TH MAY 1978

The first game of Albion's historic journey behind the 'Bamboo Curtain' to China ended with a 3-1 win over a Peking XI, Ally Brown scoring twice and Regis adding the other in front of an estimated crowd of 80,000. Elsewhere on tour, Albion beat a China XI 2-0 (Ally Brown and Regis), a Shanghai XI 2-0 (Regis and Cunningham), a Kwangtung Province XI 6-0 (Regis 2, Cunningham, Tony Brown, Wile, Martin) and a Hong Kong XI 3-0 (Regis, Tony Brown and an own goal).

SUNDAY 17TH MAY 2009

Albion were relegated from the Premier League following a 2-0 home defeat at the hands of Liverpool. At half-time, Tony Brown was presented with a plaque to commemorate his selection as Albion's representative on the 'Walk of Stars' in Birmingham's Broad Street.

SATURDAY 18TH MAY 1935

W. G. Richardson won the only England cap of his illustrious career, featuring in the 1-0 win over Holland in Amsterdam. Albion colleague Wally Boyes also made his international debut in this game, Boyes going on to play again for England, against Wales and then against the Rest of Europe.

SATURDAY 18TH MAY 1968

The Throstles won the FA Cup for the fifth time by beating Everton 1-0, Jeff Astle's goal in extra-time securing the trophy. Astle scored in every round of the competition. Dennis Clarke became the first substitute to play in an FA Cup final as he replaced the injured John Kaye at the end of the 90 minutes.

SATURDAY 19TH MAY 1888

In a game billed as being for the Championship of the World, FA Cup holders Albion headed over the border to take on Renton in Scotland, ending up well beaten, 4-1 at Hampden Park. Tom Pearson scored for Albion.

WEDNESDAY 19TH MAY 1971

Albion legend Tony Brown won his solitary England cap, against Wales at Wembley. The game ended goalless.

TUESDAY 19TH MAY 1992

The Hawthorns hosted one of its most dramatic and atmospheric nights as goals from Andy Hunt and Ian Hamilton saw the Albion overturn a 2-1 first leg deficit to beat Swansea City 2-0 in the Division Two play-off semi-final to advance to a Wembley final with Port Vale.

SATURDAY 20TH MAY 1967

While Chelsea and Tottenham were battling out the 'Cockney Cup Final' at Wembley, Albion's directors were in talks with Alan Ashman, then at Carlisle United, with a view to him replacing Jimmy Hagan at The Hawthorns. Ashman was installed as boss three days later.

THURSDAY 20TH MAY 1999

Shareholder Paul Thompson, who had quit Albion's board in February 1999, called for an EGM so "Shareholders have the opportunity to decide whether they wish Tony Hale to continue as Chairman".

FRIDAY 21ST MAY 1909

Playing against Gefle FC on the Albion's Scandinavian tour, Bill Garraty scored six goals in the 10-0 victory. Among the other games on the seven-match tour, Albion beat a Stockholm XI 8-3, Hull City 2-1 and a Swedish XI 2-0. They went down to defeat against Newcastle United, 3-0, Hull City 4-3, and a Danish XI 3-1.

FRIDAY 22ND MAY 1959

The Ontario All Stars proved to be no match for Albion who kicked off a nine-match tour of North America with a 6-1 win in Toronto, Brian Whitehouse and Bobby Robson both scoring twice, Ronnie Allen and Derek Hogg also contributed goals. Albion then drew 2-2 with Dundee in Alberta on the 24th, before beating the Alberta All-Stars 15-0 on the 27th. The rematch with Dundee on the 30th saw the Throstles win 7-1 before they finally came a cropper against the British Columbia All-Stars on June 1st, losing 3-2. Albion recorded a 10-1 win over a Manitoba XI on the 3rd, thumped Dundee 4-2 on the 6th, and then beat an Ottawa XI 9-0 on the 8th. They signed off with a 4-0 win over the Montreal All-Stars on the 10th.

SUNDAY 23RD MAY 1999

Tony Brown enjoyed a belated second Albion testimonial as the Baggies took on a Jamaican XI in front of a packed Hawthorns house of 20,356. The Reggae Boyz were ultimately victorious, scoring the only goal of the game, the likes of Bryan Robson and John Barnes in West Bromwich to pay homage to a living legend.

MONDAY 24TH MAY 1926

Joe Carter was on the mark again, scoring another goal for England in the 5-3 win over the Belgians in Antwerp. He was joined on the field by Albion goalkeeper, George Ashmore, a man who was all too often a reserve to two generations of the Pearson family, Hubert and Harold, between the sticks at The Hawthorns, in spite of being a very capable goalkeeper in his own right. This was Ashmore's only England cap.

SUNDAY 24TH MAY 1959

England were beaten in Mexico City, their hosts victorious 2-1 despite Albion man Derek Kevan once again scoring one of England's goals, putting his side ahead after 16 minutes. Team-mate Don Howe was also in the England starting line-up. England had headed across the Atlantic to assess the challenges they would face in future with an eye on the 1962 World Cup.

SUNDAY 24TH MAY 1970

In a warm-up fixture ahead of the Mexico World Cup, Jeff Astle played for an England B side against Ecuador State University and scored all four England goals in a 4-1 win to push himself further forward in Sir Alf Ramsey's thinking as England prepared to defend the Jules Rimet trophy.

SATURDAY 25TH MAY 1968

Albion followed up their FA Cup win with an often ill-tempered tour of East Africa, the African hosts apparently believing Albion were the champions of England and particularly keen to give them a beating as a result, leading to some very physical, tempestuous games. Jeff Astle scored against Tanzania to beat the hosts in the opening fixture.

WEDNESDAY 26TH MAY 1971

The mighty Internazionale of Milan were the visitors to The Hawthorns as the Anglo-Italian tournament got off the ground. John Wile got the Albion goal in a creditable 1-1 draw, but the return game in Milan saw the Throstles defeated 1-0.

WEDNESDAY 27TH MAY 1959

Bobby Robson joined a select band of players by scoring six goals in a game for Albion when he netted a double hat-trick as Alberta All-Stars were thrashed 15-0 during Albion's North American tour. Keith Smith added a hat-trick, Brian Whitehouse and Graham Williams scored two each and Joe Kennedy and Alec Jackson completed the scoring.

WEDNESDAY 28TH MAY 1952

Ronnie Allen made his England debut, playing at outside right in a friendly against Switzerland in Zurich. Nat Lofthouse scored twice and Jackie Sewell added the other in a 3-0 win.

THURSDAY 28TH MAY 1959

Derek Kevan scored his eighth and final England goal as they trounced the USA 8-1 in a friendly at Wrigley Field in Los Angeles. Bobby Charlton scored a hat-trick, Ron Flowers grabbed two and Johnny Haynes and Warren Bradley also scored. Billy Wright played his 105th and final England international.

SUNDAY 28TH MAY 1978

The Baggies were beaten 1-0 by Aalborg IF at the start of a tour of Denmark. Pride was later restored by beating a FUIN Select XI 4-1 and then an Aarhus XI, 7-0.

MONDAY 28TH MAY 2007

Hopes of an immediate return to the Premier League for the second time in a row were dashed when the Baggies were beaten in the play-off final at Wembley Stadium. Derby County, featuring ex-Albion defender Darren Moore, came through a desperately dour afternoon of football, winning by the single goal. A string of Albion players made it pretty clear afterwards that they had had enough of the Championship and wanted transfers. The supporters made it clear they'd stick with Albion.

WEDNESDAY 29TH MAY 1963

Manager Jimmy Hagan sold striker Keith Smith to his former club, Peterborough United, Hagan creating the funds necessary to bring in Terry Simpson from The Posh, and Bill Williams from Queens Park Rangers as part of his rebuilding of the club's first team.

SUNDAY 30TH MAY 1993

Albion were triumphant at the old Wembley for the last time when Ossie Ardiles' team saw off the challenge from Port Vale to win the Division Two play-off final 3-0 with goals from Andy Hunt, Nicky Reid and Kevin Donovan. Swan's dismissal for a challenge on Bob Taylor was an equally pivotal moment in the game. The game had been all-square at the half-time interval, but Albion's free flowing football proved too much for Vale to handle in the second half, the Baggies earning a fully deserved victory in a season where they scored over 100 goals. Albion fans made up around 40,000 of the 54,071 supporters in the stadium.

FRIDAY 31ST MAY 1963

John Kaye joined the Baggies from Scunthorpe United for a reported fee of £45,000, becoming Jimmy Hagan's third signing inside 48 hours. Kaye joined Albion as a centre-forward and came close to selection for England's 1966 World Cup squad in that position, but ultimately had his greatest day as a centre-half in the 1968 FA Cup-winning side, even though he was forced to come off injured at the end of 90 minutes in that game.

SATURDAY 31ST MAY 1969

For the second time inside three years, Graham Lovett was involved in a terrible car accident, this time fracturing a thigh and an arm in a collision with a bus in Quinton on his way home after Albion's return from the Palo Alto tournament in California, an accident for which he later received £1,400 in damages in court. His first accident had come at Christmas in 1966 when his car drifted off the M1 and somersaulted down the banking, Lovett lucky to survive, never mind play again. The two accidents ultimately contributed to Lovett's decision to finish playing professional football at the age of just 26.

THE ALBION
On This Day

JUNE

SATURDAY 1st JUNE 1957

Albion went behind the Iron Curtain for the first time in their history for a pioneering tour of the Soviet Union, opening up with a 1-1 draw in Leningrad against Zenit – now Zenit St. Petersburg – with Derek Kevan scoring for Albion in the stalemate.

MONDAY 1st JUNE 1981

Ron Atkinson announced that he was ready to leave the Baggies to take on the job of Manchester United manager in succession to Dave Sexton. Albion were rather less keen to see him move on given the success the club had enjoyed under his management in the previous three seasons, but the lure of the biggest club in the country eventually proved to be too much for the Throstles to combat.

TUESDAY 2nd JUNE 1964

Charles 'Chuck' Drury ended his decade-long association with the Albion by signing for Bristol City for £8,000. The Darlaston-born Drury scored one goal in his 160 senior games for Albion and played at the heart of defence alongside the likes of Stan Jones and Joe Kennedy. He made his Albion debut away at Bolton Wanderers back on February 22nd 1958.

WEDNESDAY 3rd JUNE 1981

Following secret discussions between Albion's Bert Millichip and Martin Edwards of Manchester United, the Baggies put a £200,000 transfer fee on Ron Atkinson ahead of his proposed move to Old Trafford.

FRIDAY 4th JUNE 1971

The 1970/71 season finally came to a close as the Throstles were beaten 1-0 in Cagliari in the Anglo-Italian tournament, bringing to an end a 55-game campaign that stretched back to the 0-0 draw with Crystal Palace on August 15th 1970. Tony Brown missed just one of those fixtures, the League Cup win over Charlton Athletic, 'Bomber' scoring 30 goals in his 54 appearances, topping the First Division scoring charts with 28. Jeff Astle had a positively sluggish season in comparison, scoring 16 times in 53 games.

WEDNESDAY 5TH JUNE 1968

Both Asa Hartford and Graham Williams were sent off during the tour game against East Africa, but Albion still managed a 2-2 draw with goals from Jeff Astle and Ronnie Rees.

MONDAY 5TH JUNE 1978

It was announced that Willie Johnston had failed a drugs test following Scotland's opening World Cup game with Peru in Argentina, testing positive for fencamfamine, an appetite suppressant. Scotland had slipped to a surprise 3-1 defeat in the opening fixture against Peru, a shock after the high expectations placed upon them before they left for South America when some intemperate pundits had suggested the Scots might even win the competition.

TUESDAY 6TH JUNE 1978

Willie Johnston was given a lifetime international ban by the Scottish Football Association and was sent home from Argentina after his failed drugs test. Johnston was later banned from Uefa competition too, putting him out of Albion's Uefa Cup campaign in the 1978/79 season, and hastening his departure from The Hawthorns as he lost his first team place to Laurie Cunningham.

MONDAY 7TH JUNE 1926

Harry Keys – then Albion's chairman as well as the vice-president of the Football League – was presented with a long-service medal by the Football League.

SUNDAY 7TH JUNE 1970

In England's World Cup group game against Brazil in Mexico, Jeff Astle came off the bench as a second-half substitute and within moments of arriving on the pitch, missed an opportunity to score. England were beaten 1-0 by the eventual World Cup winners, Jairzinho scoring the goal, but still comfortably qualified for the knockout phase of the competition. Astle featured from the start in the third group game, a 1-0 win over Czechoslovakia – Allan Clarke scored the winner from the penalty spot – but never played for England again after the side returned home from Mexico. He finished with five caps but no goals for his country.

SUNDAY 8TH JUNE 1958

As England got their 1958 World Cup campaign off the ground, Derek Kevan scored in the 2-2 draw with Russia in Gothenburg, Tom Finney scoring the other goal. Kevan and Albion colleague Don Howe played in all four of England's games in that World Cup series while Bobby Robson played in the first three games. To add to that, full-back Stuart Williams appeared for Wales in their 1-1 draw with Hungary.

THURSDAY 8TH JUNE 1978

Willie Johnston arrived back in the UK after being expelled from the Scotland World Cup squad in Argentina. He was greeted at Heathrow Airport by his Albion boss Ron Atkinson who jokingly suggested that he could now get a sponsorship deal with Boots following the furore over his failed drugs test. Johnston later endured an uncomfortable press conference and interview on the BBC's World Cup programme, the chief high interrogator on the drugs question being the BBC's anchor man Frank Bough.

SATURDAY 9TH JUNE 2001

One of Albion's finest ever players, Ronnie Allen, passed away in Great Wyrley at the age of 72. Once described as "the complete footballer" in his prime in the mid 1950s, Allen scored 234 goals in 415 games for the Baggies, including two goals in the 1954 FA Cup final win over Preston North End, and was the club's greatest goalscorer until his records were overtaken by Tony Brown. Allen had two spells as manager at The Hawthorns, in 1977 and then in 1981/82, and also served in other scouting and advisory capacities with the club over many years, discovering the young Cyrille Regis at Hayes.

WEDNESDAY 10TH JUNE 1981

The battle for Ron Atkinson's services came to an end as Big Ron finally left The Hawthorns for Manchester United after the two clubs had finally come to an agreement over compensation ahead of the switch. He returned later to buy Bryan Robson and Remi Moses for United amid considerable ill feeling; the controversy caused warned him off also trying to sign Derek Statham and Cyrille Regis for the Red Devils.

WEDNESDAY 11TH JUNE 1958

England played out a 0-0 draw with Brazil in Gothenburg in the 1958 World Cup, Don Howe, Derek Kevan and Bobby Robson all playing for their country against the eventual world champions in the only game that Brazil failed to win in the competition. It was following this stalemate that a youngster called Pele was introduced to the Brazilian side. Stuart Williams was also in the Welsh side that drew 1-1 with the Mexicans in Solna as both the home nations looked to progress from the group phase in the only World Cup finals where England, Wales, Scotland and Northern Ireland all qualified.

WEDNESDAY 12TH JUNE 1957

Albion played the third and final game of their tour in the Soviet Union, beating the Red Army team, CDSA, by four goals to two. Brian Whitehouse and Frank Griffin added to a brace from Derek Kevan, the only 'Tank' on show as the Throstles prevailed in front of a crowd of 80,500. The tour was pronounced a huge sporting and diplomatic success, the CDSA side repaying the compliment in due course by visiting The Hawthorns to play a game under floodlights.

FRIDAY 12TH JUNE 1981

John Wile was installed as the early favourite to replace the departing Ron Atkinson as Albion boss after he was given the job as caretaker manager, vice-chairman John Gordon announced that Wile was his favoured choice.

THURSDAY 13TH JUNE 2002

Jeremy Peace replaced Clive Stapleton as Albion's chairman, Stapleton having been acting in the chairman's role following the resignation of Paul Thompson. Peace, an Albion supporter since the 1960s, had previously been a member of the board of directors since December 8th 2000.

SATURDAY 14TH JUNE 1975

Brian Whitehouse left the Albion after a lengthy career as both a player and coach, bringing to an end his brief spell as caretaker manager in the wake of Don Howe's departure from The Hawthorns prior to the end of the 1974/75 season.

SUNDAY 15TH JUNE 1958

Derek Kevan, Don Howe and Bobby Robson were on parade for England again as the national side recorded its third successive draw, this time against the Austrians in Boras, a result that ensured they would have to go into a play-off with the USSR to decide who would progress. The final score was 2-2, Kevan and Johnny Haynes scoring for England. Once again, Stuart Williams was in action for Wales on the same day, the Welsh also drawing for a third successive game, this time 0-0 against their Swedish hosts, also ensuring they would need to take part in a play-off game.

TUESDAY 16TH JUNE 2009

Tony Mowbray left his job as Baggies boss to join Celtic. His coaching staff, Mark Venus and Peter Grant, also traded life at The Hawthorns for similar roles at Parkhead.

TUESDAY 17TH JUNE 1958

Don Howe and Derek Kevan were part of the England side defeated by the USSR in the World Cup play-off in Gothenburg, England going out of the competition after a 1-0 beating. Stuart Williams had rather better fortune as Wales won 2-1 against Hungary in their play-off fixture and so progressed to the last eight.

TUESDAY 17TH JUNE 1969

Clive 'Chippy' Clark returned to Queens Park Rangers in a player-plus-cash transfer that saw Allan Glover move north, a package deal that was estimated at being worth £70,000. Clark's career was seriously derailed when he was on the receiving end of a horrendous tackle during the Albion tour of East Africa the previous summer, Clark never again recapturing the form that had made him an Albion hero. In eight years as a quick, gutsy winger at The Hawthorns, Clark registered 98 goals in 353 games.

THURSDAY 17TH JUNE 2004

Albion right-back Bernt Haas lined up for Switzerland against England at the 2004 European Championships, but he wasn't there at the finish, dismissed for his second yellow card after an hour as the Swiss fell to a 3-0 defeat.

SATURDAY 18TH JUNE 1887

Albion headed north to play against South Shore in a friendly on the Lancashire coast and they came away with a 3-2 win thanks to goals by Billy Bassett, George Woodhall and Charlie Perry.

SATURDAY 18TH JUNE 1977

Willie Johnston was sent off while playing for Scotland against Argentina in a friendly in Buenos Aires, although the sending off was later rescinded on appeal to FIFA and no suspension followed. Sadly, things did not get any better for him when he returned to Argentina for the World Cup a year later and he was found to have failed a drugs test.

THURSDAY 19TH JUNE 1958

Stuart Williams' campaign at the World Cup ended as, just 48 hours after winning their play-off game, the Welsh came unstuck against the Brazilians, a 66th-minute goal from Pele enough to separate the two sides as Brazil went on to win the World Cup and revolutionise the game with their 4-4-2 formation in the process. Wales have never been to the World Cup again since that day, not even in the famous Andy Johnson era.

THURSDAY 19TH JUNE 1975

Johnny Giles was appointed player-manager at The Hawthorns in succession to Don Howe after lengthy negotiations. The former Leeds United midfield general was quick to stamp his passing style of football onto his team, and led them to promotion to the top flight at the first attempt, even though it took Albion a while to really get going in the new season. It took a second half of the season surge to see the Baggies race up the table to finally clinch the third automatic promotion slot on the final Saturday of the season.

MONDAY 20TH JUNE 1887

The Albion completed their brief northern tour of duty by beating Fleetwood in another friendly, 3-1, just two days after their win over South Shore. Woodhall scored twice and Harry Green was also busy troubling the scorers.

MONDAY 21st JUNE 1993

Osvaldo Ardiles officially quit as the Albion manager and was unveiled as the new boss at Tottenham Hotspur, just weeks after he had led the Throstles back into the First Division, though his assistant Keith Burkinshaw declined to accompany him. At White Hart Lane, he worked under the Spurs' chairman Alan Sugar, who later told him he was fired.

TUESDAY 22nd JUNE 1948

Jack Smith was appointed as Albion's first official manager in the modern sense, the job previously having being done by club secretaries such as Frank Heave and the legendary Fred Everiss. Smith was to enjoy early success, leading the Throstles to promotion back to the top flight in his first season, ultimately leaving to rejoin former club Reading in April 1952.

WEDNESDAY 22nd JUNE 1977

Ronnie Allen was appointed Albion manager in succession to Johnny Giles – the man who was then still the club's record goalscorer – returning to the fold having previously managed at clubs such as Wolves and Athletic Bilbao in Spain after hanging up his boots, bringing Bilbao to The Hawthorns for Bobby Hope's testimonial game in 1971. Allen still had close ties with the Throstles, working in a scouting capacity immediately prior to taking on the job as manager.

MONDAY 23rd JUNE 1913

Alf Bentley joined Albion for what was described as 'a substantial fee' from Bolton Wanderers. He went on to score an impressive 47 goals in 105 starts for the club, but lost much of his career to the Great War years. Without that hiatus, his statistics would almost certainly have been far more impressive still.

THURSDAY 24th JUNE 1993

Gary Robson ended a 12-year association with the Albion and left in the wake of the club's promotion back to Division One in order to join former coach and caretaker manager Stuart Pearson at Bradford City. His last contribution as an Albion man had been as a substitute at the Wembley play-off final win over Port Vale.

THURSDAY 25TH JUNE 1964

One of the great entertainers, Alec Jackson, left the Albion to join Birmingham City for an undisclosed fee. The Tipton-born Jackson became the youngest Albion man to score a goal when he beat the goalkeeper in his debut game at Charlton Athletic's Valley in November 1954 and was seen as a real crowd pleaser thereafter. He scored 52 goals in 208 senior games for the Throstles, but is perhaps as well known now for his role in the brilliant *The Saturday Men*, a 1962 documentary about the Baggies – on and off the field – that captured Jackson playing snooker with friends and family in his local club in Tipton. The film-makers making the point that once a man had earned riches beyond the dreams of his peers, he would never quite fit that social circle again.

TUESDAY 25TH JUNE 1968

After suffering from a dreadful tackle while on the club's end of season tour of East Africa, Clive Clark discovered the injury had been slow to heal and was told that he needed the injured ligament plastered up for a further two months and would miss the start of the new season.

THURSDAY 26TH JUNE 1969

Albion made their first ever six-figure signing by bringing Colin Suggett to The Hawthorns from Sunderland for £100,000. Along with the acquisition of Allan Glover and Danny Hegan, the Throstles spent around £200,000 in the summer of 1969 in a concerted effort to make a similar impact on league football as they had in cup football, though with no real success. Suggett started as a striker but was converted to a deeper-lying role later on by Don Howe and was perhaps playing the best football of his career when he was surprisingly sold to Norwich City for £70,000 in February 1973, having scored 30 goals in 170 senior appearances for the Throstles.

SUNDAY 27TH JUNE 1999

Chairman Tony Hale announced that he had come to agreements with local businessman Jim Driscoll and former Queens Park Rangers owner Richard Thompson that would see them join the Albion board.

FRIDAY 28TH JUNE 1963

The ranks of Albion's 'pay rebels' were swelled to six when young wing-half Ron Bradley joined Don Howe, Graham Williams, Alec Jackson, Stan Jones and Clive Clark in refusing a new contract.

SATURDAY 28TH JUNE 1969

Alan Ashman told the local press that Albion midfield-general Bobby Hope was close to agreeing a new deal with the club, his existing contract set to run out at the end of the month. Hope said, "I would like to get back to Scotland, but I will have to see what the club are prepared to offer me." Given that Hope was still involved in the Albion's scouting operation some 40 years later, the offer must have been okay.

TUESDAY 29TH JUNE 1971

It was announced that Alan Ashman had been dismissed as Albion manager. Ashman only learned of the decision when he picked up an English newspaper while on holiday after his attention had been drawn to it by a waiter who recognised his picture from the story. Speculation in the press suggested that the former Albion man Don Howe, the coach of Arsenal's 1970/71 double-winning side, was set to take charge at The Hawthorns, though all parties initially denied that this was the case.

MONDAY 30TH JUNE 1958

Len Millard left the Albion to take over as manager at Stafford Rangers, bringing to an end a 21-year spell with the club. Millard was the captain of the team that won the FA Cup in 1954 and he amassed 477 senior appearances for the club in a career interrupted by World War II.

MONDAY 30TH JUNE 1980

Danish striker Morten Skoubo was born in Struer. Skoubo enjoyed one of the briefest of any Albion career, for although he was with the club for five months as a loanee from Borussia Mönchengladbach from January to May 2004, he made just two substitute appearances, totalling a mere 22 minutes on the field.

THE ALBION
On This Day

JULY

MONDAY 1st JULY 1963

Full-back Don Howe submitted a transfer request to the Board after the Throstles refused to offer him a pay rise in the brave new world that had come into being after the abolition of the maximum wage for players two years previously. An issue that had already seen Bobby Robson leave for Fulham twelve months earlier when Albion had failed to keep up with the wages offered elsewhere in this new free market. Howe told the press; "I've made up my mind, I'm convinced it's time I made a break with Albion."

FRIDAY 2nd JULY 1993

Keith Burkinshaw was appointed Albion manager in succession to Osvaldo Ardiles having served as Ardiles' assistant in the promotion-winning season of 1992/93. It was a short-lived appointment, Burkinshaw surviving in post for little more than a year, helping keep the Baggies in the First Division with victory at Portsmouth on the final day of his only full season in charge.

SATURDAY 3rd JULY 1971

Brian Whitehouse wrote in the local *Sports Argus* that he would be leaving Arsenal in the coming days in order to rejoin the Baggies as part of Don Howe's coaching staff. There was no official announcement from the Albion on the position regarding either Whitehouse or Howe. The club was still without a manager after the sacking of Alan Ashman.

THURSDAY 3rd JULY 1975

Alan Merrick took his contract dispute with the club to the FA's Management Committee and asked them to intervene and make an adjudication on the stalemate position. He eventually left The Hawthorns in a loan move to Peterborough United in September 1975, before finally joining Kidderminster Harriers permanently in July 1976.

SATURDAY 4th JULY 1964

Manager Jimmy Hagan was linked with a move to Sheffield Wednesday, speculation strenuously denied by the Baggies who were determined to keep Hagan at The Hawthorns. Ironically, the job at Hillsborough eventually went to one of Hagan's predecessors at the Albion, Vic Buckingham, manager of the 1954 FA Cup winners.

MONDAY 5TH JULY 1920

FA Cup-winning goalkeeper Jimmy Sanders was born in Holborn, London. Sanders is perhaps still best remembered for the legendary picture of Albion's penalty at Wembley in that 1954 final, Sanders so tense he was unable to watch, instead clutching the post and looking the other way as Ronnie Allen scored from the spot at the other end. Sanders – who was a decorated hero in the RAF where he served as an air gunner during World War II, sustaining injuries that threatened to prevent him ever playing again – eventually played 364 games for the Baggies after moving north from Charlton Athletic where he was kept out of the side by Sam Bartram. He had been Albion's reserve goalkeeper for that 1953/54 season but was elevated to the first team after Norman Heath was so badly injured in a game at Sunderland that he was forced into premature retirement.

TUESDAY 6TH JULY 1971

Arsenal chairman Denis Hill-Wood condemned the ongoing Arsenal exodus to The Hawthorns as physio George Wright also decided to leave Highbury to join Don Howe's newly assembled staff in the Black Country, Howe attempting to replicate the double winning backroom at his new club. It was to be another three days before the new management was to be officially placed in situ at The Hawthorns.

WEDNESDAY 7TH JULY 1965

The Baggies kicked off an international tournament in New York by losing 2-0 to Kilmarnock at Randall's Island. That set the tone for a disastrous six-game series for Albion, a 2-0 beating of the Scots in the return game their only success. Against Hungary's Ferencvaros, the Throstles drew 1-1 and lost 2-1 and in the two matches against Polonia Byton of Poland, they managed a 2-2 draw but were also trounced 6-0.

THURSDAY 8TH JULY 1999

Following a tense EGM held at the Gala Baths in West Bromwich, Tony Hale defeated the motion to remove him and remained as the chairman of the club. He told his critics, "I have not seen or heard so much tripe since I was in a butcher's shop".

THURSDAY 9TH JULY 1959

Gordon Clark was appointed as the new Albion manager in succession to Vic Buckingham, beginning a reign of 100 league and cup games through until October 1961. Sadly, Clark failed to build on the successes of the Buckingham reign, in spite of the presence of players such as England internationals Howe, Kevan and Robson, and Albion went through a period of comparative stagnation under Clark and successor Archie Macaulay until the arrival of Jimmy Hagan shook things up.

FRIDAY 9TH JULY 1971

Don Howe was finally officially named as the new Albion manager, before taking up his duties with the club on July 12th. Howe's tenure saw the Baggies relegated from the top division for the first time in a quarter of a century as the Albion careers of such big names as Jeff Astle, Bobby Hope, Graham Williams and John Kaye were ended, perhaps prematurely in some cases.

TUESDAY 10TH JULY 1900

Tom Pickering became the first player to be signed by Albion after the announcement of their move from Stoney Lane to The Hawthorns. Pickering had previously played his football for Brierley Hill Alliance, but the Wednesbury-born man failed to make the transition to a higher class of football, scoring just twice in 10 games for the Albion before moving on to Kettering Town.

SATURDAY 11TH JULY 1981

England international Peter Barnes declared that he had undergone a change of mind, withdrawing his demand to be allowed to leave the Baggies and agreeing to stay after discussions with newly appointed manager Ronnie Allen, back at The Hawthorns for a second spell after the departure of Ron Atkinson.

FRIDAY 11TH JULY 2003

Two new signings were announced as Albion looked to bounce back to the Premier League at the first attempt. Stoke City's James O'Connor, a midfield ball winner, and striker Rob Hulse of Crewe Alexandra, joined the Throstles for a combined fee said to be in the region of £1 million as the Baggies bolstered their squad.

DON HOWE STARTED WORK AS ALBION MANAGER WITH THIS SQUAD OF PLAYERS ON 12TH JULY 1971

MONDAY 12th JULY 1971

After a prolonged transitional period, played out largely on the back pages of the newspapers, Don Howe finally arrived for his first day at the office at The Hawthorns, taking charge as manager of the Albion. Addressing the players on their return for pre-season training, he announced his ambitions to the playing staff, dreams which allegedly included; "making the blue and white stripes as famous as the white of Real Madrid."

TUESDAY 13th JULY 1999

John Gorman was appointed assistant to Albion boss Denis Smith as the dust settled after the stormy EGM a week earlier. Gorman was initially installed only in a temporary role after leaving the FA's employ when Glenn Hoddle was sacked as the England manager, Gorman having been acting as Hoddle's assistant. Smith told local reporters that he hoped that Gorman would go on to join him on a permanent basis, although the inevitable speculation was that Gorman was simply biding his time until Hoddle took on another managerial appointment elsewhere.

TUESDAY 14th JULY 1998

Amid a hectic pre-season period under Denis Smith, Albion engaged in seven friendlies in just 14 days, the first of which was a 3-2 win over Worcester City with Kevin Kilbane, Tony Dobson and Micky Evans scoring the goals for the Baggies.

WEDNESDAY 14th JULY 1999

Albion ended speculation about Lee Hughes' future at the club by announcing that the striker had signed a new contract that was intended to keep him at the club until June 2002. It later transpired that he had inserted a get-out clause into that contract that allowed him to leave Albion if any club tabled a bid in excess of £5 million, as Coventry City later did in the summer of 2001.

On the same day, the Baggies busied themselves by playing a friendly in Greve on their pre-season tour of Norway. Kevin Kilbane knocked in two goals, Micky Evans and Adam Oliver adding others as the Albion romped to a 4-0 victory. Three days later, Albion were defeated in their other tour game, losing 2-1 to Odense.

SATURDAY 15TH JULY 1989

Laurie Cunningham met his tragically early end when he was killed in a car crash near Madrid at the age of just 33. Cunningham was one of the most naturally gifted footballers who ever set foot on The Hawthorns turf: graceful, elegant, with sublime balance, glue-like close control and incredible acceleration. The first black footballer to represent England at under-21 level, he also played for England's senior side while with the Throstles. He, perhaps, left this country just a year too early when he headed for Real Madrid in the summer of 1979 after alerting the Spanish giants to his gifts with a majestic performance in Valencia in the Uefa Cup of 1978/79. His transfer to Spain for £900,000, along with Len Cantello's switch to Bolton Wanderers under the new freedom of contract arrangements, saw the beginning of the break up of the finest Albion side since the cup-winning years of 1954 and 1968. For Cunningham, a string of injuries meant he never really fulfilled his potential in Madrid and found himself playing for a number of other clubs, including a brief spell at Manchester United, and another at Wimbledon, where he won an FA Cup winner's medal as substitute when the Crazy Gang beat Liverpool.

TUESDAY 16TH JULY 1963

The board were forced to meet to discuss player unrest at the club in the wake of Jimmy Hagan's arrival as manager. Don Howe, Graham Williams, Alec Jackson and Ron Bradley were all unsettled, while Hagan said; "The position with these players will be discussed at the meeting. This will be the first opportunity we have had to thrash things out." Hagan gradually resolved the disquiet over the following twelve months by shipping the majority of those who disagreed with him out of The Hawthorns.

SATURDAY 17TH JULY 2004

Planning for the second crack at the Premier League began to hot up when Gary Megson signed Birmingham City defender Darren Purse for £750,000. A wholehearted competitor, it's safe to say that, unfortunately, Purse did not go on to enjoy the best time of his career at The Hawthorns and was on his way to Cardiff City a year later after falling out of favour under the new Bryan Robson regime.

SATURDAY 18TH JULY 1992

Baggies fans got their first sight of Albion under Ardiles as Ossie took his team to play against non-league Evesham, drawing a crowd of 2,338 fans. The Throstles were comfortable winners, 4-0, goals coming from Gary Robson, Bob Taylor and Bernie McNally as well as an own goal.

FRIDAY 19TH JULY 1963

It was announced that the club were going to build a cantilever stand on the Birmingham Road side of The Hawthorns at the cost of £50,000, as well as a reduction in ground capacity of 5,000 that brought its own further reaching financial implications. In addition, Albion promised to make further improvements to the Halfords Lane Stand including refurbishing the dressing rooms and improving the catering and toilet facilities for supporters.

SATURDAY 20TH JULY 2002

The Baggies played two different friendlies on the same day prior to heading to the south coast to prepare for the first season in the Premier League. One of the Albion XIs were beaten 2-0 in disappointing fashion at Halesowen Town, while those who played against Bromsgrove Rovers fared rather better, coming out 6-1 winners thanks to a hat-trick from Scott Dobie, two from Jason Roberts and another from Matt Turner.

WEDNESDAY 21ST JULY 1965

In an effort to beat the heat and oppressive humidity in the Big Apple, Albion endured one of the latest kick-off times in our history, beginning the New York International Tournament game with Ferencvaros at 9.15 pm local time. Despite the respite from the heat, the Baggies were beaten 2-1 by the Hungarian side in front of 5,663 supporters.

MONDAY 22ND JULY 1974

Jeff Astle left Albion and signed for Dunstable Town, then managed by Barry Fry. In the following season, the King scored 34 goals and took Dunstable to promotion to the Southern League Premier Division. In his Albion career, Astle had registered 174 goals in 361 games, including, most memorably, the goal that won the 1968 FA Cup final against Everton.

THURSDAY 23RD JULY 1964

Former Walsall stalwart Albert McPherson was appointed coach at The Hawthorns by Jimmy Hagan, McPherson leaving his post at non-league Stourbridge Town to take on his new opportunity.

THURSDAY 24TH JULY 1997

Taking part in the Isle of Man Festival Trophy, the Baggies successfully overcame the first hurdle by defeating Port Vale in the opener, Andy Hunt and Bob Taylor scoring without reply. The Baggies went on to lift the trophy by beating Bury 1-0 in the final.

THURSDAY 25TH JULY 1963

After submitting his transfer request at the beginning of the month, full-back Don Howe was once again at loggerheads with manager Jimmy Hagan, the manager insisting that the club "cannot afford to let Howe go at this time". In those days before the introduction of freedom of contract, Howe could not simply move to another club without the Albion's say so, as players are able to do in the post-Bosman world, and so was retained on a month-by-month contract, on terms with which he was patently dissatisfied. Howe remained at The Hawthorns through almost all of the 1963/64 season, featuring in 35 more Division One games and four in the FA Cup.

SUNDAY 25TH JULY 1965

Albion's pre-season visit to the United States came to a close with a thumping defeat against the Polish side Polonia Byton. The Baggies were thrashed 6-0 at Downing Stadium, Randall's Island, though in mitigation, the kick-off time of 2.30 pm in searing heat and humidity did them few favours. Jeff Astle was later heard to say; "We couldn't wait to get on the plane home." And this from someone who was terrified of flying.

SATURDAY 25TH JULY 1992

In a sign of things to come, Ossie Ardiles' Albion continued pre-season preparations by scoring seven goals to win their friendly at St. Albans City, the non-leaguers unable to find a goal in reply. That meant the Throstles had rattled in a dozen goals without conceding in their three opening friendlies under the Argentine.

SATURDAY 26TH JULY 1981

Ronnie Allen was installed as the manager at The Hawthorns for a second spell following the departure of Ron Atkinson to Manchester United – the man who had replaced him after Allen himself had left The Hawthorns for a coaching role in Saudi Arabia. Allen led the Throstles to two cup semi-finals in the season, but a disastrous league campaign only saw Albion escape relegation at the death, and Allen was moved upstairs into a General Manager's role after just a season in charge of the team.

TUESDAY 27TH JULY 1982

Former Aston Villa player and coach Ron Maurice Wylie was appointed the Albion's new manager after Ronnie Allen was shuffled upstairs into the job of general manager at the end of the 1981/82 campaign. Wylie was a rather dour figure and with memories of the champagne years under Ron Atkinson still vivid in the memories of supporters, his reign at The Hawthorns was always destined to be brief and unpopular, not least because of his ties with Witton. Wylie lasted just 80 games at the helm.

TUESDAY 27TH JULY 1999

One of the club's less glorious pieces of news management… A press statement was issued to announce the appointment of Jim Driscoll to the board of directors and then, following notes about other matters of largely internal interest, it was announced that team manager Denis Smith was leaving the club, just three weeks after his position had been apparently reaffirmed at the EGM. Chairman Tony Hale commented; "The Board recognises that performances on the pitch must improve. We have decided that a new manager must be appointed and we are seeking that appointment ASAP."

FRIDAY 28TH JULY 1972

A pre-season tour of Sweden got underway with a comfortable 3-0 victory over Kalmar. Bobby Gould scored twice and full-back Gordon Nisbet added a third. In a broadly successful tour, the Baggies went on to enjoy a win over Helsingborg, Gould adding two more goals to one from George McVitie as they won 3-1. The final tour game against Lanskroner was drawn 1-1 with Tony Brown getting the goal.

TUESDAY 29TH JULY 1902

Albion's 19-year-old assistant secretary, Fred Everiss, was given a promotion, replacing the recently departed Frank Heaven as the club's secretary, a decision that came about through the unanimous acclamation of the board of directors who commended his work as a stop-gap in that position over the previous couple of months since Heaven's resignation. Everiss went on to become one of the great figures in Albion history.

WEDNESDAY 30TH JULY 1969

A reshaped Albion, boasting new signings Allan Glover, Danny Hegan and Colin Suggett, headed for Norway as part of pre-season preparation to play two games in two days. The first of these was played in Bergen against a Norwegian under-23 XI, the Baggies defeated 3-2 by the cream of young Scandinavian talent, though Hegan started his Albion career by scoring both the goals. The following day, Albion took on SK Lyn in Oslo and got a rather better result, a thumping 6-0 win. Jeff Astle weighed in with a hat-trick, Bobby Hope scored twice and Percy Freeman added the other, his only first team goal for Albion.

THURSDAY 30TH JULY 1992

The Throstles played their first ever game against opposition from the newly constituted Premier League when Sheffield Wednesday arrived at The Hawthorns. Bob Taylor and Kwame Ampadu were the goalscorers as Albion achieved a creditable 2-2 draw in front of a crowd of 6,171 fans, eager to see the first fruits of the Ardiles revolution after the Bobby Gould interregnum.

SATURDAY 31ST JULY 1971

Don Howe's Albion began the new campaign in earnest by beating Wrexham 2-1 in Wales in the Watney Cup first round tie, Tony Brown getting both goals, one of them from the penalty spot.

SATURDAY 31ST JULY 1999

Coventry City granted Cyrille Regis a testimonial game at Highfield Road and the Albion were the appropriate visitors, the Baggies beaten 4-2 by their Premiership rivals, Daryl Burgess and Micky Evans getting the goals for the visitors in front of 5,739 supporters.

THE ALBION
On This Day

AUGUST

WEDNESDAY 1st AUGUST 1979

In a spirit of reciprocation after the Albion had been the first English team to visit China in 1978, the Chinese national side was welcomed to The Hawthorns for a friendly fixture. The Throstles were far too strong for their opponents, however, running out 4-0 winners with goals from Ally Brown, Cyrille Regis and Peter Barnes, along with an own goal. The second half of the game was screened live on BBC2.

TUESDAY 1st AUGUST 2000

The formalities around the signing of Derek McInnes were finally completed and he was immediately installed as the captain of Gary Megson's team. A former Rangers midfielder who had played for Megson while on loan at Stockport County, McInnes went on to play 100 games for the Throstles, scoring six goals and leading the side to promotion to the Premier League in 2001/02, before returning to his native Scotland with Dundee United.

SATURDAY 2nd AUGUST 1969

The Baggies got in a little more important pre-season preparation, with the big kick-off just seven days away, by travelling up to Millmoor and beating Rotherham United 4-0 in a friendly, the goals coming from new signings Allan Glover and Danny Hegan plus another from Jeff Astle and an own goal from the Millers.

MONDAY 2nd AUGUST 1976

Crewe Alexandra were put to the sword as Albion geared up for a return to the top flight under Johnny Giles with a trip up to Gresty Road. The Baggies came home after a 6-2 victory with Ally Brown getting a brace, Len Cantello, Tony Brown, Joe Mayo and Gordon Nisbet doing the rest of the damage.

WEDNESDAY 2nd AUGUST 1978

The English phase of the Anglo-Scottish tournament opened with Albion taking on Mansfield Town at The Hawthorns. It took an absolute screamer of a goal from Len Cantello to give Albion a draw in front of a crowd of 5,704. Albion failed to progress from their group, beating Hull City 2-1 but losing 2-1 to Leicester City, both games away from home.

SATURDAY 3RD AUGUST 1968

FA Cup holders Albion took on the First Division champions, Manchester City, in the FA Charity Shield game at Maine Road. Albion goalkeeper John Osborne injured a finger during the game and had to be replaced by skipper Graham Williams between the posts, just as he had been in the fourth round cup-tie at Southampton in Albion's successful FA Cup run. Things did not go quite so well on this occasion as Albion were thrashed 6-1 by Joe Mercer's team. Dick Krzywicki scored the consolation goal for the travelling Baggies.

FRIDAY 4TH AUGUST 1905

The 1905/06 season started in inauspicious fashion as even before a ball was kicked the club's offices were broken into by thieves. It was discovered that the only items that had been taken were 12 shirts, belonging to the players.

WEDNESDAY 4TH AUGUST 1971

Albion secured their passage to the Watney Cup final by beating Halifax Town 2-0 up in Yorkshire, Colin Suggett scoring both of the goals as Don Howe had his sights set on winning a trophy within the first month of taking up his job as the manager.

SATURDAY 5TH AUGUST 1978

The Baggies were in Scotland to defend the Tennent Caledonian Cup in a competition held at Rangers' Ibrox Stadium, a four-team competition. In the semi-final game, the Baggies fell at the first hurdle, losing a penalty shootout 3-1 after a 1-1 draw with Southampton, Cyrille Regis scoring the Albion goal in normal time. Albion misery was compounded the following afternoon when they lost the third-place play-off to Heart of Midlothian, 2-0.

SATURDAY 5TH AUGUST 2006

John Hartson marked his Albion debut by scoring twice against Hull City as the Throstles got off to a winning 2-0 start under Bryan Robson in their first season in the second tier under the 'Championship' moniker. Sadly, that was to prove the highlight of Hartson's period at The Hawthorns, which came to a halt midway through the 2007/08 season.

SATURDAY 6TH AUGUST 1977

Albion were triumphant in a see-saw game in the Tennent-Caledonian Cup at Ibrox, Bryan Robson, David Cross, and two from Tony Brown, the four goals that saw them edge past St. Mirren into the final, beating the Buddies 4-3 in front of a crowd of 40,404.

FRIDAY 6TH AUGUST 2004

The Throstles pulled off one of the greatest transfer coups in the history of the club by signing Nwankwo Kanu from Arsenal, the Nigerian joining the Baggies on a Bosman move after being unable to command a regular starting place under Arsene Wenger at Highbury.

SATURDAY 7TH AUGUST 1971

The final of the Watney Cup was held at The Hawthorns, the Throstles welcoming lowly Colchester United in what, it was assumed, would be a straightforward victory. 19,009 supporters turned up in expectation of seeing Albion lifting the trophy. In an enthralling game, the contest ended up at 4-4 with two strikes from Jeff Astle and other goals from Len Cantello and Colin Suggett taking things to a first ever penalty shootout at The Hawthorns. Albion were beaten 4-3, allowing Colchester skipper, and former Baggies full-back and penalty specialist, Bobby Cram to pick up the trophy. Sadly, it was all downhill after that in the Don Howe era.

SUNDAY 7TH AUGUST 1977

Pitted against home team Rangers in the final of the Tennent-Caledonian Cup, Albion were inspired by Willie Johnston, back at the club where his career started, and Laurie Cunningham who scored twice as they collected their first piece of silverware under Ronnie Allen, winning 2-0.

SATURDAY 8TH AUGUST 1964

The Baggies began a three-match tour of Holland by taking on AZ Alkmaar, but were defeated by two goals to one, Clive Clark on the mark for Albion. Things did improve over the rest of the trip, however, Tony Brown and Doug Fraser guiding Albion to a win over ADO and then Bobby Hope's goal proving enough to beat the rapidly emerging Ajax in Amsterdam.

THURSDAY 9TH AUGUST 1962

Bobby Robson left the Albion to go back to his old club Fulham after a dispute over wages that had rumbled on for some six months, during which time Robson had continued to play for England and had travelled to the 1962 World Cup, injury denying him a place in the team. He was replaced by the young Bobby Moore. Fulham paid £20,000 for Robson, only £5,000 less than the Throstles had spent on acquiring him from Craven Cottage six years before.

SATURDAY 9TH AUGUST 1969

Colin Suggett made an emphatic debut for the Albion, scoring twice as the Throstles defeated Southampton 2-0 at The Dell in the opening game of the season. Danny Hegan and Percy Freeman also made their first team debuts for the club, but did not trouble the scorers.

FRIDAY 10TH AUGUST 1900

A number of 5% debentures were issued by the club in order to help finance the cost of converting a Staffordshire meadow that was to be found at the corner of the Birmingham Road and Halfords Lane. We now know that meadow as The Hawthorns.

SATURDAY 11TH AUGUST 1979

The Throstles celebrated their centenary with a special game against Ajax, captained by the Dutch World Cup star Ruud Krol. Fittingly enough, Albion triumphed over the then three times European Cup winners, new signing Peter Barnes' goal enough to separate the two teams.

THURSDAY 11TH AUGUST 1994

The club announced that Tony Hale would take over as the new chairman at the following month's AGM when the sitting chairman, Trevor Summers, would resign from the post.

WEDNESDAY 11TH AUGUST 1999

Brian Little was finally confirmed as the Albion manager, the replacement for Denis Smith. Little was unable to take up the role prior to this day given outstanding contractual agreements with Stoke City, his previous club, which would have required the Baggies to pay out £50,000 in compensation.

SATURDAY 12TH AUGUST 2000

A reshaped Albion under Gary Megson were defeated 1-0 at Nottingham Forest's City Ground in the first game of the new season. Derek McInnes and Jason Roberts both made their senior debuts for the club in the defeat.

SUNDAY 13TH AUGUST 1978

Tony Brown scored against one of the more unusual opponents in his career, the Damascus Police XI, in order to earn a 1-1 draw on a short tour of Syria – it probably made good diplomatic sense not to go one further and actually beat the police.

TUESDAY 14TH AUGUST 1900

Still looking to foot the bill for the conversion of The Hawthorns, Albion's Board decided to issue a further number of 5% debentures to the value of £600, bringing the total value issued to £1,800.

WEDNESDAY 14TH AUGUST 1968

The reigning European champions, Manchester United, were beaten at The Hawthorns by the FA Cup holders in the first home game of the new season; the Throstles 3-1 victors with Jeff Astle scoring twice and Tony Brown adding the other one. The biggest league crowd of the season at The Hawthorns, 38,299, were in attendance.

SATURDAY 14TH JULY 1971

Don Howe got off to a winning start as the Albion manager when his side collected a 1-0 victory at West Ham United's Upton Park, Tony Brown getting the goal. Victory in the second game promised much, but the Throstles failed to live up to those lofty early hopes.

SATURDAY 14TH AUGUST 2004

Attempting to take on the Premier League for the second time, Albion's season opened with a 1-1 draw at Blackburn's Ewood Park, Neil Clement scoring for Albion. Another very different looking side took to the field after a summer of transfer activity, Jonathan Greening, Nwankwo Kanu, Ricci Scimeca and Darren Purse all making their debuts from the start, Zoltan Gera joining them as a substitute.

WEDNESDAY 15TH AUGUST 1900

The club secretary, Frank Heaven, was informed that the patch of land that the Albion were busily converting into a football ground on the Birmingham Road had once been the site of an estate called The Hawthorns, as it had once been bordered with a hawthorn hedge. Heaven told the board of directors that the name should be reintroduced for the as-yet-unnamed ground. Records suggest "there was some mirth" when the name was first suggested, but it was quickly adopted and remains the somewhat poetic name of the stadium to this day.

THURSDAY 16TH AUGUST 1979

Having already lost Laurie Cunningham and Len Cantello from the fine side of the previous season – both transferred out of the club – Albion's plans for the new term were thrown into further disarray when Cyrille Regis was seriously injured in a friendly with Honved in La Coruna, Spain. Speculation suggested he would be sidelined for around two months, though in fact it was late November before he got a starting place in the team again.

SATURDAY 16TH AUGUST 1997

Striker Lee Hughes made his Albion debut in the 3-2 win at Crewe Alexandra's Gresty Road, Hughes scoring twice. Andy Hunt added the other from the penalty spot.

SATURDAY 16TH AUGUST 2003

Macedonia international Artim Sakiri – 'the Beckham of the Balkans' – made his first ever appearance for the Baggies and scored a sensational goal from 30 yards against Burnley in the 4-1 victory at The Hawthorns, the undoubted high spot of an otherwise troubled time with the club. Rob Hulse scored twice and Lee Hughes got the other one.

SATURDAY 17TH AUGUST 2002

Albion played their first-ever fixture in the Premier League, going north to take on Manchester United at Old Trafford, watched by a crowd of 67,645 in bright sunshine. Albion's day out was spoiled when Derek McInnes was given a red card for a second-half tackle, and then late on when Solskjaer won the match for the hosts.

SATURDAY 18TH AUGUST 1962

Another opening day at Old Trafford, Albion ending up with a valuable 2-2 draw against Manchester United thanks to goals by Derek Kevan and Keith Smith.

SATURDAY 18TH AUGUST 2001

The new East Stand was in use for the first time as Albion were defeated 1-0 by Grimsby Town at The Hawthorns, Bob Taylor missing a penalty in the game. Missed penalties were to be something of a motif all season long until the penultimate game when Igor Balis scored from the spot at Bradford City to give Albion one foot in the Premier League.

SATURDAY 18TH AUGUST 2007

Loanee Ishmael Miller made his Albion debut as a second-half substitute against Preston North End and within moments went on a surging run before scoring a goal reminiscent of Cyrille Regis to get the crowd on its feet. The goal sealed a 2-0 victory for the Baggies.

SATURDAY 19TH AUGUST 1939

With the war rapidly approaching, Albion and Aston Villa played a special game in aid of the Football League Jubilee Fund at Villa Park, W. G. Richardson scoring in the 1-1 draw.

SATURDAY 19TH AUGUST 1978

One of the finest seasons in recent times got under way when Albion defeated Ipswich Town 2-1 at The Hawthorns, Ally Brown getting things off to the best possible start of scoring the first goal of the game after just 21 seconds.

SATURDAY 20TH AUGUST 1949

Winger George Lee made his debut for the Throstles after moving from Nottingham Forest for £12,000. Lee was on the winning side as a goal from Cyril Williams was sufficient to see off Charlton Athletic at The Hawthorns. Lee played 295 games for the Albion, including the 1954 FA Cup final, and scored 65 goals before leaving in June 1958. He returned to The Hawthorns in the early 1960s to work as coach to the youth side.

IGLESIAS BORJA VALERO BECAME THE THROSTLES' MOST EXPENSIVE SIGNING WHEN HE JOINED FROM REAL MALLORCA ON 22ND AUGUST 2008

TUESDAY 21st AUGUST 1900

At an Albion Board meeting, the directors chose to push the boat out with the inaugural game on the new ground in the offing. They decreed that the club should purchase "one dozen jerseys and one dozen knickers" so that their players could be immaculately turned out come the big day. It was reported at the same meeting that the playing surface was in beautiful condition ahead of the first game, to be played just a fortnight later against Derby County.

SATURDAY 21st AUGUST 1948

Jack Smith took charge of his first game as Albion's gaffer – the first official manager in the history of the Baggies – and led them to a 1-0 win at Nottingham Forest, Dave Walsh getting the critical goal. It was a portent of good times ahead, Albion ending the season by getting promoted back to the top flight.

FRIDAY 22nd AUGUST 2008

Albion smashed their existing transfer record with the purchase of Iglesias Borja Valero from Real Mallorca in Spain. The midfield playmaker made the move to England for a reported figure of £4.7 million after having featured for his club side in a friendly at The Hawthorns just a fortnight earlier and was immediately thrown into the first team just four days later, in a League Cup tie at Hartlepool United – the very definition of culture shock.

THURSDAY 23rd AUGUST 1883

One of the true handful of legends in West Bromwich Albion history, Jesse Pennington, was born in West Bromwich. A skilful full-back for club and country, a true sportsman in every sense of the word, Pennington became a byword for playing the game in the right fashion.

THURSDAY 23rd AUGUST 1984

Sir Bert Millichip stepped down as a director of the club, almost a year to the day after resigning as chairman, but was elected president, a position he held until his death.

WEDNESDAY 24th AUGUST 1955

Derek Kevan and Don Howe both made their Albion debuts as the Baggies saw off Everton with a 2-0 victory at The Hawthorns, Kevan celebrating his call-up by scoring both of the goals, beginning one of the most prolific goalscoring careers in Albion history.

SATURDAY 24th AUGUST 1963

A mixed afternoon for Albion saw them come away from a home game with Leicester City with a 1-1 draw, Ronnie Fenton scoring. John Kaye and Terry Simpson both made their debuts for the Throstles, but Bobby Hope had to leave the field with a nasty injury that put him out for the rest of the season, a three-game comeback in mid season proving abortive.

SATURDAY 25th AUGUST 1928

Albion were in good form as the 1928/29 season started, Clapton Orient sent back off to London after a 3-1 hiding, Harry Chambers, Tommy Glidden and Joe Carter all on the scoresheet.

WEDNESDAY 25th AUGUST 2004

The Hungarian international Zoltan Gera celebrated his first start for the club by scoring in the 1-1 draw with Tottenham Hotspur at The Hawthorns, unleashing his trademark somersault celebration after the goal had gone in. It was the third successive 1-1 draw as the season opened for the Albion.

FRIDAY 26th AUGUST 1983

Sir Bert Millichip stood down as chairman of the Albion, citing the pressure of his commitments at the Football Association as the decisive factor. He continued as a director of the club.

SATURDAY 26th AUGUST 2000

In what became something of a tradition under Gary Megson, Albion crowned a miserable start to the season by slipping to their third straight defeat of the campaign, thoroughly outplayed at Oakwell as Barnsley claimed a 4-1 victory. Albion gradually turned things round, however, and ended the season in the play-offs after finishing sixth, eventually going down to defeat against Bolton Wanderers.

SATURDAY 27TH AUGUST 1927

Jimmy Cookson made his Albion debut and scored in the 3-1 defeat at Oldham's Boundary Park. Cookson's career stats at The Hawthorns are simply unbelievable, 117 goals in 131 senior appearances before he left for Plymouth Argyle six years later. Cookson later returned to the Throstles as a scout and made an equally important contribution – it was Cookson who spotted the great Ray Barlow and recommended him to the Baggies.

TUESDAY 27TH AUGUST 2002

The Throstles were given a real introduction to what life in the Premier League was all about as they were played off the park at Highbury by Arsenal who produced football of a level and intensity that Albion had not encountered in 20 years. The Gunners seemed able to score almost at will and most Baggies fans were happy to see the side retreat back up the M1 having only lost 5-2.

SATURDAY 28TH AUGUST 1954

The Baggies proved they meant business in the season ahead by bouncing back from losing their first two games to beat Arsenal 3-1 at The Hawthorns with strikes from Ronnie Allen, Paddy Ryan and Johnnie Nicholls. Albion then went on a nine-match unbeaten run, of which seven were wins, to put them back in the title picture after having finished second the season before, form which petered out in mid season.

SATURDAY 29TH AUGUST 1931

Albion's first game back in the top flight after winning promotion was against Arsenal at Highbury but a goal from Stan Wood in front of a massive crowd of 52,478 saw the Baggies beat the eventual First Division runners up. Albion fielded the same XI that had won the FA Cup against Birmingham City at Wembley some four months earlier.

SATURDAY 29TH AUGUST 1942

Len Millard made his Albion debut in a wartime game, though that did not go on to form part of his 'official' career statistics. The Baggies beat Northampton Town 2-0 in a Football League North fixture.

SATURDAY 30TH AUGUST 1941

Harry 'Popeye' Jones was in dead-eye form in front of goal, rattling in four as Albion marched on to a 6-3 victory over Cardiff City in the Football League South. Billy Elliott and Jack Johnson completed the scoring.

WEDNESDAY 30TH AUGUST 1967

New boss Alan Ashman finally collected his first win with the Throstles at the fourth attempt, Albion rising to the derby occasion and simply crushing Wolves 4-1 at The Hawthorns, in front of a crowd of 38,373. Jeff Astle, Clive Clark, Kenny Stephens and John Kaye were the goalscorers but it proved a false dawn as Albion won just that one game in their first seven and were dumped out of the League Cup by Third Division Reading. The normally placid Ashman then read his players the riot act and an upturn in fortunes swiftly followed.

MONDAY 31ST AUGUST 1903

Harry Keys resigned as the chairman after a critical letter from his directors was printed in the local press. In spite of that, his resignation was not fully accepted by the directors until October 29th 1903.

WEDNESDAY 31ST AUGUST 1910

Former player Dan Nurse was elected to the Albion's board of directors as the replacement for the retiring Charles Couse.

SATURDAY 31ST AUGUST 1946

The Football League finally resumed after the cessation of hostilities in World War II, Albion getting things off on the front foot by beating Swansea Town 3-2 at the Vetch Field, Dave Walsh scoring twice on his debut. Frank Hodgetts contributed the other goal.

WEDNESDAY 31ST AUGUST 1977

Cyrille Regis appeared in the Albion shirt for the first time, replacing the injured Tony Brown as the Throstles took on Rotherham United in the League Cup. Regis scored twice and was immediately given cult status by the supporters as Albion completed a routine 4-0 win, John Wile and Mick Martin added the other goals.

THE ALBION
On This Day

SEPTEMBER

MONDAY 1st SEPTEMBER 1930

The Baggies showed they would be a force to be reckoned with by visiting Charlton Athletic and winning 4-0 with goals from Jimmy Cookson, Stan Wood, Henry Boston and an own goal. It was part of a real statement of intent at the opening of the campaign as Albion reeled off four straight wins.

SATURDAY 1st SEPTEMBER 1973

The Throstles played their first Second Division game at The Hawthorns in 25 years, and maintained their 100% record for the season by beating Crystal Palace, who had been relegated with them the previous season, thanks to an Allan Glover goal. This followed a 3-2 win at Blackpool on the opening day of the season. Unfortunately, the early season promise soon petered out.

SATURDAY 1st SEPTEMBER 1979

The dismal opening to Albion's centenary season continued when, after taking just one point in their first three games, they were beaten 5-1 at The Hawthorns by European champions Nottingham Forest. That thumping left Albion at the foot of the table having finished third the year before. Fortunately, results did pick up and the Baggies finished the season in 10th place in the top division.

TUESDAY 1st SEPTEMBER 2009

Dutch under-21 international Ryan Donk beat the transfer deadline to sign for the Albion on a season-long loan from AZ Alkmaar, joining Dutch colleague Gianni Zuiverloon, another summer signing, in the Albion dressing room ahead of the Premier League campaign.

SATURDAY 2nd SEPTEMBER 1905

A publishing institution was born with the issue of the first-ever Albion match programme for the game against Burnley. A crowd of 7,223 watched the Baggies lose 2-1.

SATURDAY 2nd SEPTEMBER 1972

Tony Brown clocked up his 300th league appearance for the club in the 1-0 defeat at Everton's Goodison Park. There were still another 274 league appearances to come from the Bomber.

MONDAY 3RD SEPTEMBER 1900

One of the most significant days in Albion history, The Hawthorns staged its first-ever game, with a crowd of 20,500 turning up to take it in. The opponents were Derby County who had the temerity to take the lead through the great England striker Steve Bloomer. Albion ensured there was a happy ending of sorts by coming back to equalise through 'Chippy' Simmons.

THURSDAY 3RD SEPTEMBER 1987

Ron Atkinson returned to the Albion for a second spell in charge as manager, desperately trying to halt the slide that had seen the Baggies drop out of the top flight and plummet in the direction of Division Three. Atkinson managed to get things on a more even keel, largely by drafting in experienced players such as Andy Gray and Brian Talbot.

SUNDAY 3RD SEPTEMBER 2000

Albion celebrated 100 years at The Hawthorns by going one better than in the first game, beating Crystal Palace 1-0 thanks to Derek McInnes' first goal for the club. The crowd had fallen by nearly 7,000 since that first game, though given it was 100 years on, it's surprising more of them weren't dead.

SATURDAY 4TH SEPTEMBER 1965

Jeff Astle scored his first hat-trick for the Albion, John Kaye adding the other in a 4-2 win over Sheffield Wednesday. Six days later, Astle added a second as the Throstles won 4-3 at Northampton Town in the Cobblers' only First Division season.

WEDNESDAY 4TH SEPTEMBER 1974

Succeeding Jim Gaunt, Bert Millichip took over as chairman of the Albion, a post he was to hold for nine years.

SATURDAY 4TH SEPTEMBER 1982

Albion continued a bright start with a 3-1 win over Manchester United, much to the delight of the home crowd who were happy enough to see Ron Atkinson, Bryan Robson and Remi Moses on the losing side. Martyn Bennett, Ally Brown and Peter Eastoe all scored.

MONDAY 5TH SEPTEMBER 1910

One of the early greats at The Hawthorns, defender Joe Smith made his debut for the Throstles against Bolton Wanderers. It wasn't the best of starts as his team slipped to a 3-1 defeat, but Smith recovered from that early reverse to go on to play 471 games for the club either side of World War I.

SATURDAY 5TH SEPTEMBER 1970

Jesse Pennington passed away in Kidderminster Hospital at the age of 87. Pennington was one of the great pioneers of the club in his playing days and is remembered to this day. There is a suite named in his honour in the East Stand at The Hawthorns.

SATURDAY 5TH SEPTEMBER 1981

After a sluggish start to the season following the summer departure of manager Ron Atkinson and the upheaval that had gone on around it, Albion found their best form by thrashing Swansea City 4-1 with a hat-trick from Cyrille Regis and another from Steve Mackenzie. It was a fitting performance as this was also the day that the club officially opened the reconstructed Halfords Lane Stand.

SUNDAY 5TH SEPTEMBER 1993

Darren Bradley scored an absolute scorcher from 30 yards as the Throstles recovered from going behind to beat Wolverhampton Wanderers 3-2 in a proper blood and thunder derby game played out in front of the TV cameras. Paul Raven and Kevin Donovan also scored, Donovan counting out the goals in celebration in order to assist anyone in the crowd who wasn't aware of the scoreline. It was also the last time supporters were allowed to stand at The Hawthorns for a game against the Wolves.

SATURDAY 6TH SEPTEMBER 1913

Striker Alf Bentley etched his name into Albion history by becoming the only Albion player ever to score four goals on his debut, the feat coming against Burnley as the Baggies strolled to a 4-1 home win. Bentley ended up with 17 goals for the club in a career interrupted by the Great War.

WEDNESDAY 7TH SEPTEMBER 1966

They haven't always had huge crowds at Newcastle United, for only 24,748 were there to watch Albion give the home side a lesson in a convincing 3-1 win over the Toon, the goals coming from John Kaye and Clive Clark, who scored twice.

SATURDAY 8TH SEPTEMBER 1888

The Football League came into existence and Albion were pitted against Stoke City at Stoney Lane on the first day. Albion won 2-0 with goals from Joe Wilson and George 'Spry' Woodhall. Had goal difference or goal average come into existence at that stage, the Throstles would have topped the first-ever Football League table. As it was, no method for separating clubs on equal points had yet been decided, so Albion were merely joint top.

SATURDAY 8TH SEPTEMBER 1894

There was an early thrashing for the Wolves as the Throstles took their local rivals apart at Stoney Lane, winning 5-1 just seven days before they were to beat Liverpool 5-0 on the same ground. Roddy McLeod, Billy Richards, Billy Bassett, Billy Newall and Tommy Hutchinson all scored as the goals were shared around against Wolverhampton.

SATURDAY 8TH SEPTEMBER 1962

Derek Kevan had a field day against Fulham by blasting in four goals in the 6-1 win at The Hawthorns, Keith Smith adding two more as Kenny Foggo made his debut for the club. Kevan was on his way to topping the scoring charts for Albion for the sixth season running, even though his campaign was curtailed when he was sold to Chelsea in the following March.

SATURDAY 8TH SEPTEMBER 2001

Kevin Keegan's Manchester City were on the wrong end of a pasting as Albion belatedly found their form after a slow start to the season, winning 4-0 at a canter. Derek McInnes laced one in from the edge of the box, Neil Clement scored twice, and Scott Dobie added another in a dominant performance. Both teams were promoted at the end of the season.

SATURDAY 9TH SEPTEMBER 1939

The Throstles played their final league game prior to the cessation of normal football for the duration of World War II. Eric Jones signed off with a hat-trick, but Albion still lost, 4-3 to Tottenham Hotspur at The Hawthorns.

SATURDAY 9TH SEPTEMBER 1972

At the eighth attempt, Albion posted their first win of the season by beating the reigning champions, Brian Clough's Derby County, 2-1 at The Hawthorns. Bobby Gould and Tony Brown scored the critical goals as the Baggies floundered at the bottom of the division.

SATURDAY 9TH SEPTEMBER 1989

Goals from Chris Whyte, Don Goodman and Colin West saw the Baggies register a first win of their season after the first four games had yielded just two points. Leicester City were the obliging victims in a 3-1 win at Filbert Street.

SATURDAY 10TH SEPTEMBER 1949

Once in a blue moon, Albion get a result at Stoke, and this was such a day. The Baggies triumphed with a 3-1 victory over the Potters, Cyril Williams getting two of the goals, Jack Haines weighing in with the other.

SATURDAY 10TH SEPTEMBER 1966

Fulham were beaten out of sight at The Hawthorns by a rampant Albion who won 5-1 with a brace from both Bobby Hope and Clive Clark, and another from Jeff Astle.

TUESDAY 11TH SEPTEMBER 2001

Amid the eeriest of atmospheres following the terrorist attacks on the World Trade Center, Albion played out a League Cup tie with Swindon Town, and won 2-0 in extra time with goals from Jordao and Scott Dobie. The authorities insisted the tie go ahead as opposition fans were already travelling to the game when the atrocities took place. Albion's players were actually training on The Hawthorns in the afternoon when the pictures began to come in from New York and later watched the news as it unfolded from within the ground.

SATURDAY 12TH SEPTEMBER 1964

Two penalties helped Bobby Cram towards a hat-trick against Stoke City as the Baggies came out on top against the Potters with a 5-3 win. Cram became, it is believed, only the second full-back ever to score a hat-trick in English league football, following on from Birmingham's Stan Lynn six years before. Tony Brown and Kenny Foggo scored Albion's other goals.

WEDNESDAY 13TH SEPTEMBER 1978

Albion were back in European competition for the first time in a decade, for their first crack at the Uefa Cup. The first game was out in Turkey, at Galatasaray, in a stadium which has since become infamous for its "Welcome to Hell" banners. The Throstles found it far less intimidating, strolling to a 3-1 win, with two goals from Laurie Cunningham and another from Bryan Robson making the second leg little more than a formality. No English side won again at Galatasaray until Chelsea did so in the Champions League in October 1999.

SATURDAY 13TH SEPTEMBER 2008

Tony Mowbray's Albion recorded their first win in the Premier League with a 3-2 victory over West Ham United. The game was notable for neither side having a shirt sponsor; Albion played all season without one, West Ham having lost theirs when the company involved went out of business just ahead of the fixture, the logo covered up by a claret patch on their shirts. In a pulsating game, James Morrison scored after just three minutes; West Ham were 2-1 up by the 35th minute before a Roman Bednar penalty brought things level before the break. Chris Brunt won the game for the Throstles with a clinical finish seven minutes from time, Scott Carson producing a last gasp save to preserve the three points.

WEDNESDAY 14TH SEPTEMBER 1966

Albion began the defence of the League Cup by smashing Aston Villa at The Hawthorns in the second round tie. The 6-1 scoreline matched Albion's competition record achieved against Coventry City the previous season, and featured a hat-trick from Bobby Hope, two from Doug Fraser and another goal from Clive Clark in front of a crowd of 25,039.

TUESDAY 15TH SEPTEMBER 1885

After working their way through a succession of increasingly garish colour combinations at the Annual General Meeting, it was decided that henceforth, Albion would wear blue and white stripes as their colours. That was a good day's work well done.

SATURDAY 15TH SEPTEMBER 1979

Finally putting their early season woes behind them, Albion gave Malcolm Allison's expensively reshaped Manchester City a good thrashing and recorded their first win of the season to the tune of four goals to nil. City 'reject' Gary Owen was well pleased to be on the scoresheet against his old club, while the other goals came from Bryan Robson, Ally Brown and Kevin Summerfield.

SATURDAY 15TH SEPTEMBER 2007

Just to prove that football really is a funny old game after all, the Throstles spent much of the 90 minutes against Ipswich Town under the cosh, but still came away as 4-0 winners after having scored three times in the last three minutes. Ishmael Miller, Filipe Teixeira and a brace from Kevin Phillips did the damage to the Tractor Boys.

SATURDAY 16TH SEPTEMBER 1922

Albion got some quick revenge over Aston Villa when, just a week after losing at Villa Park, they beat them 3-0 at The Hawthorns, Stan Davies scoring twice, Fred Morris getting the other one.

WEDNESDAY 16TH SEPTEMBER 1953

The Throstles recorded their biggest ever win at Newcastle United on a famous afternoon when the Geordies were annihilated 7-3 by an Albion team at its absolute peak. Johnnie Nicholls scored three, Ronnie Allen added two more and Frank Griffin and Paddy Ryan helped themselves as well to round off the scoring. A crowd of 58,075 were there to witness it, the highest away crowd of the season. Ironically, the visit of Newcastle in round five of the FA Cup generated the best attendance at The Hawthorns, 61,088. Only the FA Cup semi-final against Port Vale at Villa Park (67,977) and the final itself against Preston North End at Wembley (100,000) topped that figure.

SATURDAY 17TH SEPTEMBER 1927

Jimmy Cookson became the only Albion player ever to score six goals in a league fixture as he posted a double hat-trick in the 6-3 win over Blackpool at The Hawthorns. It was a vintage season for Cookson who scored 38 goals in the league, also a record for the Baggies, though that was to be surpassed in 1935/36 when W. G. Richardson managed 39.

SATURDAY 17TH SEPTEMBER 1966

Albion were defeated but got plenty of glory from an amazing game at Everton's Goodison Park as they were defeated 5-4 by the Toffees in a rollercoaster game. Jeff Astle, Doug Fraser, Bobby Cram and John Kaye scored for Albion as Everton clinched victory at the death following a stirring fightback by the Throstles.

WEDNESDAY 18TH SEPTEMBER 1957

The Hawthorns staged its first game under floodlights as Albion took on Chelsea in front of 36,835 fans. The game ended in a 1-1 draw, Ronnie Allen enjoying a moment in the spotlight as he scored a penalty.

WEDNESDAY 18TH SEPTEMBER 1963

Doug Fraser made his debut for the Baggies just 24 hours after he'd been signed from Aberdeen by Jimmy Hagan. He featured in the 3-1 derby win at home to Birmingham City, Kenny Foggo, Clive Clark and Alec Jackson scoring the goals.

WEDNESDAY 18TH SEPTEMBER 1968

A tempestuous night in Belgium saw the Throstles beaten 3-1 by RFC Bruges in the first leg of their European Cup Winners' Cup tie, a game that entered folklore as the 'Battle of Bruges'. Asa Hartford scored for the Albion but the evening was marred by riots off the field and attacks on the players as they tried to leave the pitch. Bruges were also a pretty physical outfit and Jeff Astle in particular received some special treatment from their defenders. Albion turned the tie around on home soil though, Hartford and Tony Brown scoring in the 2-0 win as the Baggies progressed on the away goals rule.

SATURDAY 19TH SEPTEMBER 1925

Torrential rain caused the home fixture with Bury to be abandoned after 51 minutes, the visitors two goals to the good at the time. When the game was replayed on November 9th, the Baggies ran out easy winners, 4-0, Stan Davies getting two, Arthur Fitton and Joe Carter adding the others.

SATURDAY 19TH SEPTEMBER 1953

Charlton Athletic visited the Black Country and inflicted a 3-2 defeat on the Albion, the first time that Vic Buckingham's XI had been beaten that season, in their tenth game, Ray Barlow and Frank Griffin scoring the goals. The Baggies responded smartly to the reverse, winning the next five matches on the spin.

SATURDAY 19TH SEPTEMBER 1959

Leeds United were dismissed out of hand, 3-0, at The Hawthorns as two goals from Ronnie Allen and another from Bobby Robson proved more than enough to send them on their way. Leeds were relegated at the end of the season.

SATURDAY 20TH SEPTEMBER 1919

The Throstles completed a second victory over Everton inside a week. Having won 4-3 at The Hawthorns seven days earlier, they were even more emphatic victors at Goodison Park, winning 5-2 with Andy Smith and John Crisp both getting two goals, Claude Jephcott getting the other one. Everton had been the last champions of England before the outbreak of war. Albion were to become the first after the return of peace.

TUESDAY 20TH SEPTEMBER 1904

Former Albion player Jem Bayliss was elected as chairman at a meeting of the Board. The meeting convened to discuss Albion's finances that, at the time, were in disarray.

SATURDAY 20TH SEPTEMBER 1975

Geoff Hurst scored his second and last goal for the Baggies as part of his brief spell with the club under Johnny Giles. It came in the 1-1 draw with Charlton Athletic at The Hawthorns. Hurst played just 12 times for Albion.

SATURDAY 21st SEPTEMBER 1957

Albion recorded their biggest-ever win at The Hawthorns, trouncing Manchester City by nine goals to two, with 26,222 there to see it. Frank Griffin scored a hat-trick, Don Howe got two and Brian Whitehouse, Bobby Robson, Derek Kevan and Roy Horobin finished the job.

SATURDAY 21st SEPTEMBER 1968

A stuttering Albion began to find a little form with a 0-0 draw against Wolves at The Hawthorns, a welcome result in a weak opening to the season that was to see them bow out of the League Cup to lowly Peterborough United just four days later.

SATURDAY 21st SEPTEMBER 2002

Goalkeeper Joe Murphy made his Albion debut, coming on as a substitute after Russell Hoult was red carded early on in the game against Liverpool at Anfield. Murphy's first touch of the ball came as he saved a penalty from Michael Owen, but he couldn't prevent the Albion from going down to a 2-0 defeat at the finish.

SATURDAY 22nd SEPTEMBER 1888

A first-ever Football League defeat, in Albion's third game of the inaugural season, came at the hands of Blackburn Rovers who beat the travelling Throstles 6-2, Tommy Pearson and Jem Bayliss scoring the consolation goals.

SATURDAY 22nd SEPTEMBER 1962

A nine-goal thriller ended up in Albion's favour as they finally prevailed over Bolton Wanderers, 5-4 at The Hawthorns. Derek Kevan was in fine form, getting three, Kenny Foggo and Don Howe chiming in too.

WEDNESDAY 22nd SEPTEMBER 1965

The Baggies played their first-ever League Cup tie having hitherto refused to enter the competition. Walsall were the visitors to The Hawthorns in a local derby, Albion coming out on top with a 3-1 win thanks to two goals from Tony Brown and an own goal from Stan Bennett, father of future Albion stalwart Martyn. The supporters certainly had an appetite for the competition – 41,188 turned up to watch.

WEDNESDAY 23RD SEPTEMBER 1931

The Baggies went to Maine Road and handed out a beating to Manchester City, winning 5-2 with two goals from Harry Raw, another from Tommy Glidden – Stan Wood and W. G. Richardson also contributed. Albion made a fine start to their first season back in the top flight after the promotion and FA Cup double season, losing just two of their first 11 games.

SATURDAY 23RD SEPTEMBER 1950

Burnley were beaten in the Black Country, George Lee and Dave Walsh scoring the goals that saw their side to a 2-1 victory.

WEDNESDAY 23RD SEPTEMBER 1981

In his final appearance of any description in Albion colours, Tony Brown played for the reserves at Blackpool's Bloomfield Road as the Baggies went down to a 2-0 defeat. The crowd of 196 was something of a contrast to rather bigger crowds he had previously played in front of.

MONDAY 24TH SEPTEMBER 1888

In a move that was some 60 or 70 years ahead of its time, the Throstles took on Walsall Town Swifts at Walsall in a match billed as being played "under electric lights" – an early version of the Walsall Illuminations. Tom Pearson and Billy Bassett scored for Albion in the 2-2 draw.

SATURDAY 24TH SEPTEMBER 1932

After four wins and two draws in their opening half a dozen games, Albion tasted defeat for the first time that season when they lost out to a single Leeds United goal at The Hawthorns. Albion maintained their solid form through the campaign and finished fourth in Division One. W. G. Richardson scored 30 goals.

SATURDAY 24TH SEPTEMBER 1960

Another hat-trick for Ronnie Allen, his last one for the Albion, set his team on the way to a 6-3 win over Manchester City at The Hawthorns, Derek Kevan knocking in a brace and David Burnside also putting one in the onion bag.

'MR ALBION', TONY BROWN MADE HIS FINAL APPEARANCE FOR THE BAGGIES, IN THE RESERVES AT BLACKPOOL ON 23RD SEPTEMBER 1981

SATURDAY 25TH SEPTEMBER 1954

In something of a goal festival, Albion came out on top 6-4 against Leicester City at The Hawthorns, with Johnnie Nicholls scoring a hat-trick, his last for the club. Frank Griffin, George Lee and Ronnie Allen found the back of the net too.

SATURDAY 25TH SEPTEMBER 1982

Big Cyrille Regis was at the top of his game as Albion made the lengthy journey to Norwich City, Regis banging in a hat-trick as Norwich City were well beaten, 3-1, in their own back yard. The slump in attendances that went on through the 1980s was reflected in a crowd of just 14,404.

THURSDAY 25TH SEPTEMBER 2008

The luckless Neil Clement was told that for the third season running, he would need a knee operation after picking up an injury in pre-season, though at least this was not on the same knee that had caused him to miss the bulk of the previous two campaigns. Clement ultimately missed the whole of the 2008/09 season because of the injury.

SATURDAY 26TH SEPTEMBER 1903

Jesse Pennington made his league debut for the Albion in a 3-1 win against Liverpool at Anfield, the crowd totalling 15,578. 'Chippy' Simmons, Alf Hobson and George Dorsett scored the goals. Seventeen years later, Pennington was still going strong as he captained the Throstles to their only ever league title.

SATURDAY 26TH SEPTEMBER 1981

Jack Vernon's death in his native Belfast was announced by the *Sports Argus*. The centre-half is still regarded by many who saw him as the finest ever to play for the Albion, despite only being at The Hawthorns for five years just after the war.

SATURDAY 26TH SEPTEMBER 1992

Goals from Ian Hamilton and Bernie McNally saw the Baggies maintain top spot in Division Three as life under Osvaldo Ardiles continued to go smoothly, Exeter City beaten 2-0 at The Hawthorns. The victory over the Grecians meant Albion had accumulated 22 points out of the first 27 available to them.

WEDNESDAY 27th SEPTEMBER 1978

Albion finished the job of beating Galatasaray in the Uefa Cup, repeating the 3-1 scoreline of the first leg in handing out a defeat at The Hawthorns, with Laurie Cunningham, Bryan Robson and John Trewick applying the nails to the Turkish coffin.

SATURDAY 27th SEPTEMBER 2008

The Throstles won their first – and only – away game of the Premiership season by beating Middlesbrough 1-0 at the Riverside Stadium, defender Jonas Olsson getting the only goal of the game.

SATURDAY 28th SEPTEMBER 1895

Goals from Billy Bassett and two from winger Jack Paddock put a stop to a run of four defeats in a row at the start of the season, Nottingham Forest seen off 3-1 at Stoney Lane. It was to be a dreadful season as the Baggies didn't win again for another seven games and won just six times all season as they finished bottom. Fortunately, there was no relegation as the Baggies survived via the end of season 'Test' matches against Liverpool and Manchester City, an early version of the play-off concept that saw Small Heath (Birmingham City as they now are) relegated and Manchester City fail to win promotion.

SATURDAY 28th SEPTEMBER 1946

The great Ray Barlow made his Albion debut, playing at inside-left against Newport County at Somerton Park in a 7-2 victory in which he scored his first goal for the club. Barlow was to make his name at left-half where he became one of the very finest footballers that the Albion ever produced. In total, Barlow played 449 senior games for the Throstles, scoring 36 times.

SATURDAY 28th SEPTEMBER 1963

Tony Brown played his first game for the Baggies and, inevitably perhaps, got on the scoresheet in the 2-1 victory over Ipswich Town at Portman Road. Perhaps the greatest club man in the history of the football club, Bomber ended up by playing 720 games and scoring 279 goals for the Albion, a true legend in his own lifetime.

WEDNESDAY 29TH SEPTEMBER 1954

The Baggies travelled to Molineux to take part in the FA Charity Shield fixture against Wolves. A crowd of 45,035 paying £4,599 enjoyed an epic game that ended up at 4-4 with Ronnie Allen registering a hat-trick, Paddy Ryan scoring the other one. The two clubs shared the Charity Shield for six months each.

WEDNESDAY 30TH SEPTEMBER 1964

In a hectic day, Jeff Astle signed for Albion from Notts County and then took his place on the field for his debut at Leicester City as the Baggies were beaten 4-2. Astle turned up in the dressing room wearing a green blazer so John Kaye assumed that he was the new bus driver for the team coach.

SATURDAY 30TH SEPTEMBER 1978

Tony Brown was on the mark in the 3-1 win at Chelsea's Stamford Bridge to equal Ronnie Allen's league goalscoring record of 208 goals. John Wile and Cyrille Regis also scored in the victory.

WEDNESDAY 30TH SEPTEMBER 1981

Albion were beaten 3-1 at home by Grasshoppers Zurich in the second leg of their Uefa Cup tie, giving the Swiss side a 4-1 aggregate win, Ally Robertson scoring the only goal for the Throstles. The defeat paved the way for Bryan Robson to move to Manchester United, who had been courting him ever since Ron Atkinson had moved to Old Trafford that summer.

MONDAY 30TH SEPTEMBER 1985

Johnny Giles ended his second spell as Albion manager, resigning his post in the aftermath of the 3-0 defeat at Coventry City's Highfield Road. The Baggies had made a catastrophic start to the season, drawing the opening-day fixture at home to newly promoted Oxford United and then losing the next nine in a row, culminating with the loss to the Sky Blues. Giles was initially replaced by Nobby Stiles as caretaker manager, Ron Saunders eventually taking over on a permanent basis. Or on as permanent a basis as any Albion manager in the turbulent 1980s and 1990s.

THE ALBION
On This Day

OCTOBER

SATURDAY 1st OCTOBER 1892

Albion took to the field against a side called Newton Heath for the first time in a Football League game, the Stoney Lane fixture ending in a goalless draw. In the return fixture a week later, the Baggies were triumphant, 4-2, the first of a series of high scoring games down the years against the club that was to become better known as Manchester United.

SATURDAY 1st OCTOBER 1921

Charles 'Tug' Wilson became the youngest player, at the time, ever to turn out for the Baggies when he made his debut in a 1-0 defeat at Oldham Athletic at the tender age of 16 years 63 days.

THURSDAY 1st OCTOBER 1981

The prolonged chase for Bryan Robson's signature ended when it was announced that he was ready to join Manchester United for a British record transfer fee of £1.5million. The formalities concluded the following day when he signed his contract on the pitch at Old Trafford. Remi Moses also went to join United in the course of the transfer saga, though Moses moved under the freedom of contract regulations.

SATURDAY 2nd OCTOBER 1976

Bryan Robson broke his leg against Tottenham Hotspur in a game at The Hawthorns, on an afternoon that was dramatic in every sense as the Throstles fought back from 2-0 down at half-time to win 4-2 with two goals from Mick Martin, a Tony Brown penalty and another from Ray Treacey. Robson fought back from the injury to play again before the season ended, only to then break his leg for the second time in the 2-0 defeat at home to Manchester City on April 16th 1976.

SATURDAY 2nd OCTOBER 2004

The Baggies won their first Premier League game of the season, at the eighth attempt, beating Bolton Wanderers 2-1 at The Hawthorns through goals from Nigeria's Nwankwo Kanu and Zoltan Gera of Hungary. It proved to be Albion's final win under Sheffield's Gary Megson, who left the club three weeks later.

SATURDAY 3RD OCTOBER 1914

In the final season before the Great War, Albion won 4-1 at Bradford Park Avenue. The goals came from Alf Bentley, two from Fred Morris and another from Harold Bache. Bache did not return from the front. He was killed in action, in France, in 1916.

SATURDAY 3RD OCTOBER 1953

Freddie Cox, who had joined the Baggies as a player-coach after a distinguished career at both Tottenham and Arsenal, made his debut in the 2-1 home win over Middlesbrough in which George Lee and Johnnie Nicholls got the goals. Cox made just four first team appearances for Albion.

SATURDAY 3RD OCTOBER 1970

Albion mounted a strong comeback to grab a 2-2 draw against Ipswich Town at Portman Road having been 2-0 down. The old firm of Tony Brown and Jeff Astle got the goals that won a point.

SATURDAY 4TH OCTOBER 1902

The Throstles came back from Molineux with two points in tow after they beat Wolves 2-1 in a Division One game, George Dorset and 'Chippy' Simmons scoring the goals for the Albion.

WEDNESDAY 4TH OCTOBER 1989

After being beaten 3-1 at home in the first leg of their second round League Cup tie, the Baggies went up to Bradford City with little hope of making progress. But a 5-3 win on the night meant that Albion went through on away goals, the aggregate score locked at 6-6. John Thomas scored a hat-trick for the visitors, Brian Talbot and Chris Whyte adding the others to ensure Albion would make the trip to Newcastle United in the next round.

SATURDAY 4TH OCTOBER 2008

A 61st-minute goal from Roman Bednar gave the Baggies a second successive Premier League win, and their third in four games, as they defeated Fulham by a single goal at The Hawthorns, pushing the Throstles into the top half of the table.

SATURDAY 5TH OCTOBER 1901

The long since defunct Gainsborough Trinity were hurried on their way to last place in the Second Division by a thumping 7-0 defeat at the hands of the Throstles at The Hawthorns as the Albion were on the charge towards the title. Tom Worton scored twice, as did 'Chippy' Simmons. 'Scottie' Smith, Jimmy McLean and Billy Lee completed the magnificent seven.

THURSDAY 5TH OCTOBER 1950

Albion director – and former player – Claude Jephcott passed away at his home in Penn, just 26 days short of his 59th birthday. The Smethwick-born Jephcott had had his career ended after breaking a leg against Aston Villa in 1922, having collected a league champion's medal in 1919/20, and been on the losing side in the 1912 FA Cup final.

WEDNESDAY 5TH OCTOBER 1966

Kenny Stephens marked his Albion debut with a goal, scoring in the 4-2 win over Manchester City in the third round League Cup tie at The Hawthorns. Dick Krzywicki, Jeff Astle and Clive Clark were also on the mark.

SATURDAY 5TH OCTOBER 1985

The Baggies ended a nine-match losing streak in the First Division by drawing 1-1 with Tottenham Hotspur at The Hawthorns bringing their points tally to two after 11 games. Carl Valentine scored the goal that offered a glimmer of hope that the season might be salvaged.

SATURDAY 6TH OCTOBER 1934

W. G. Richardson helped himself to four goals in the 6-3 hammering of Leeds United at The Hawthorns, Richardson receiving goalscoring support from Wally Boyes and Joe Carter.

WEDNESDAY 6TH OCTOBER 1982

A disastrous trip to Nottingham Forest's City Ground saw Albion incur their worst-ever beating in the Football League Cup, going down to a 6-1 hammering from Bran Clough's side, Cyrille Regis scoring the only goal for the Baggies. Honour was marginally restored in the second leg which Albion won 3-1 at The Hawthorns, to lose 7-4 on aggregate.

WEDNESDAY 7TH OCTOBER 1931

FA Cup holders Albion travelled to Villa Park to take on the reigning champions, Arsenal, in the FA Charity Shield game, only to be beaten 1-0 in front of a small crowd of 21,276 who paid £1,279 in receipts.

SATURDAY 7TH OCTOBER 1972

Albion's biggest crowd of the season, 39,309, saw two goals from Ally Brown earn the Baggies a draw against Manchester United. The trip to Old Trafford later in the campaign drew the biggest away gate of the season, 46,738.

SATURDAY 8TH OCTOBER 1904

A hat-trick from George Dorsett, allied to a goal from Lawrie Bell, gave the Throstles a convincing 4-0 win over Burton United at The Hawthorns, having won their previous home fixture 6-1 against Doncaster Rovers with another Dorsett hat-trick. Injury cut short Dorsett's contribution to the campaign, leaving him with seven goals from 13 appearances.

SATURDAY 8TH OCTOBER 1932

A thorough, some might say righteous, beating was dispensed to the team from Wolverhampton as W. G. Richardson knocked in two, Teddy Sandford and Tommy Glidden topping off the 4-1 thrashing in front of a Hawthorns crowd of 30,058.

SATURDAY 9TH OCTOBER 1965

Goalkeeper Dick Sheppard made his debut for the Baggies against Sunderland at The Hawthorns, a thoroughly satisfactory occasion for all concerned. He was beaten just the once while Albion stuck four in the Rokermen's net, two goals coming from Tony Brown and others from John Kaye and Bobby Cram.

SATURDAY 9TH OCTOBER 1971

Goals from Bobby Gould and Tony Brown defeated Crystal Palace at Selhurst Park, bringing an end to a horrible run of nine First Division games without a win. It hardly represented the turning of a corner – Albion then went ten more games before they picked up another victory, surprisingly in the Christmas fixture with Liverpool.

SATURDAY 10TH OCTOBER 1953

Huddersfield Town were the wrong team in the wrong place at the wrong time as they found themselves well beaten by a rampant Albion as Ronnie Allen registered a hat-trick and Johnnie Nicholls another in the Albion's 4-0 win at The Hawthorns. A fortnight later, Allen knocked in another three as Chelsea were shown out of town with only a 5-2 defeat to hang on to.

SATURDAY 10TH OCTOBER 1964

Jeff Astle began his goalscoring career for the Throstles with two against Wolves in the 5-1 thumping of the local rivals at The Hawthorns. John Kaye also scored twice, Bobby Cram adding another.

SATURDAY 10TH OCTOBER 1970

Despite struggling towards the bottom of the First Division, the Throstles managed to record a creditable 2-2 draw with the all-conquering Leeds United side at The Hawthorns, Colin Suggett and new signing George 'The Wing' McVitie knocking in the goals.

WEDNESDAY 10TH OCTOBER 1984

Albion supporters were shocked when the club accepted a bid for Cyrille Regis… The striker was allowed to move across the Midlands to Coventry City for the paltry sum of just £300,000. Cyrille went on to win an FA Cup winner's medal with the side from Highfield Road.

SATURDAY 11TH OCTOBER 1958

As part of a triumphant season on the road, the Throstles made the short trip to Villa Park and handed out a 4-1 beating to the Villans; Dave Burnside, Derek Hogg, Bobby Robson and Don Howe giving the Baggies a first league win at Villa Park in 23 years. Albion won ten times on the road in the 1958/59 season, drawing a further five games.

SATURDAY 11TH OCTOBER 1986

A rare day of cheer in another bleak campaign, Albion won 1-0 at Blackburn's Ewood Park, Paul Dyson scoring. Dyson played in all of Albion's 46 games that season.

THURSDAY 12TH OCTOBER 1961

Manager Gordon Clark resigned after a succession of poor results left the Throstles fourth from bottom of the First Division. Press speculation had Archie Macaulay and Jimmy Hagan as the forerunners among the potential replacements. Ironically, both got the chance to manage the Albion, and in that order.

TUESDAY 12TH OCTOBER 1999

Albion went down to their first defeat under Brian Little, some 14 games into the campaign, as they were beaten 2-1 by Fulham in the League Cup at The Hawthorns. That included nine league games, but only two had been won. The number of draws rather than wins ultimately cost Little his job.

SATURDAY 13TH OCTOBER 1900

In a grim relegation season, the Throstles suffered the first of two successive 6-1 defeats, this one at Bury, 'Chippy' Simmons getting the goal. A week later, Nottingham Forest came to The Hawthorns and administered six of the best, Amos Adams scoring for Albion.

WEDNESDAY 13TH OCTOBER 1954

In a wonderful exhibition game, Albion were finally beaten 5-3 by the Hungarian champions Honved in Brussels, in front of a crowd of 55,000. Honved, fielding many of the players who had been in the Hungarian side which had beaten England 6-3 at Wembley just a year earlier, were given a fierce examination by the Throstles, but were just too strong in the finish. Johnnie Nicholls scored twice and Ronnie Allen got the other Albion goal.

WEDNESDAY 13TH OCTOBER 1965

Albion continued their progress in the first round of the League Cup, winning in convincing fashion at Elland Road, beating Leeds United 4-2 with strikes from Tony Brown, John Kaye, Clive Clark and Jeff Astle.

THURSDAY 13TH OCTOBER 1988

Following the departure of Ron Atkinson as manager, former Ipswich Town and Arsenal midfielder Brian Talbot was appointed caretaker manager of the club as they struggled to hold on to a position in Division Two.

SATURDAY 14TH OCTOBER 1922

Albion posted their best-ever victory over Arsenal, handing out a crushing 7-0 beating to the Gunners at The Hawthorns. Freddie Morris was on target on four occasions, John Crisp scored twice and Howard Gregory also added a goal. It was some revenge after Albion had lost 3-1 at Highbury seven days earlier.

SATURDAY 14TH OCTOBER 1978

Tony Brown became the first Albion player to score 209 league goals, breaking Ronnie Allen's previous record, by getting one of Albion's goals in the 3-1 win over Leeds United at Elland Road. Cyrille Regis scored the other two Baggies goals.

SATURDAY 14TH OCTOBER 2006

With newly appointed manager Tony Mowbray waiting in the wings ready to take over, the Throstles turned on the style in an effort to impress the new man, dismantling Ipswich Town to the tune of five goals to one. Kevin Phillips scored a hat-trick and Dio Kamara added two more as the Baggies proved simply too good for the Suffolk side.

SATURDAY 15TH OCTOBER 1921

Albion defeated their near neighbours Aston Villa on their own patch in front of a huge crowd of 55,000. Bobby Blood scored the only goal of the game for the Baggies to collect the points.

TUESDAY 15TH OCTOBER 1985

With Johnny Giles having resigned from his position as Albion boss, World Cup winner Nobby Stiles took charge as caretaker manager. Stiles made it very clear that he had no interest in taking the job on full time, leaving Albion to search for a more permanent replacement.

SATURDAY 15TH OCTOBER 1988

Brian Talbot's spell as caretaker boss started on an emphatic winning note as the Throstles smashed Birmingham City at St. Andrew's, Robert Hopkins getting two against his former club and Gary Robson and Stewart Phillips also chipping in as Blues were bashed 4-1.

KEVIN PHILLIPS SCORED A HAT-TRICK IN THE 5-1 WIN OVER IPSWICH TOWN AT PORTMAN ROAD ON 14 OCTOBER 2006

SATURDAY 16TH OCTOBER 1897

Albion were victorious up at Sunderland, beating the eventual runners up in the First Division by two goals to nil, thanks to an own goal and another from Billy Bassett.

SATURDAY 16TH OCTOBER 1976

To celebrate the club's 3,000th league game, and with the inspiration coming from player-manager Johnny Giles – who set the tone with a glorious goal from 25 yards – Albion thumped Manchester United 4-0 at The Hawthorns. Ally Brown, Len Cantello and Ray Treacey completed the scoring in a the game captured by the BBC's *Match of the Day* cameras.

TUESDAY 16TH OCTOBER 2001

Bob Taylor scored his first goals of the season some twelve games into the campaign as the Baggies produced a solid performance to beat Stockport County on their own patch, 2-1. Former Albion hero Richard Sneekes featured for the home side in this game and got a standing ovation from the travelling Albion crowd when he left the field.

SATURDAY 17TH OCTOBER 1959

Both full-back Bobby Cram and goalkeeper Jock Wallace – later to find fame as manager of Glasgow Rangers – made their debuts for the Baggies, in a goalless draw at Bolton Wanderers' Burnden Park.

SATURDAY 17TH OCTOBER 1964

Young Gerry Howshall scored the first of his three Albion career goals to beat Aston Villa 1-0 at Villa Park in front of a thin crowd of 26,091. That completed a good week for the Albion having whacked the Wolves in another local derby, 5-1, just seven days earlier.

TUESDAY 17TH OCTOBER 2000

In a televised fixture, Albion came out on top against Wolves at The Hawthorns thanks to a Lee Hughes penalty. Wolves were reduced to ten men when Smith was red carded in the second half, the Throstles full value for the win in which James Chambers starred as a makeshift right-back, having played at sweeper earlier in the season.

SATURDAY 18TH OCTOBER 1958

Goalkeeper Ray Potter made the first of 238 appearances for the Throstles in a 2-1 win over West Ham United at The Hawthorns with the goals coming from Jimmy Campbell and Don Howe.

WEDNESDAY 18TH OCTOBER 1978

Albion went out to Portugal for the first leg of a second round Uefa Cup tie with SC Braga, and returned with a very comfortable lead in the bag. Two Cyrille Regis goals separated the teams.

SATURDAY 19TH OCTOBER 1935

A 7-0 win at Villa Park, secured on this day, remains Albion's biggest margin of victory over the Witton side, W. G. Richardson going on the rampage to score four times. Stan Wood, Jack Sankey and John Mahon completed the rout.

THURSDAY 19TH OCTOBER 1961

Speculation over the future of the playing side of the club ended with the appointment of Archie Macaulay as the new Albion boss in succession to Gordon Clark. Macaulay had been a Scottish international during a playing career interrupted by war, playing for clubs such as Rangers and Arsenal. He joined Albion after leaving his post as manager at Norwich City where he had some success, notably as FA Cup giant-killers.

SATURDAY 19TH OCTOBER 1968

Digging themselves out of early season trouble, Albion posted a fourth win in a row by beating Arsenal at The Hawthorns thanks to a Tony Brown goal.

SATURDAY 19TH OCTOBER 1985

Finally, at the 13th attempt, Albion won a league game in the dismal 1985/86 season. Birmingham City were beaten 2-1 at The Hawthorns with goals from Carl Valentine and Imre Varadi. Nobby Stiles was caretaker boss at the time after Johnny Giles had left the club almost three weeks earlier. Albion were relegated at the end of the campaign, by which time Ron Saunders had taken over as manager. Unsurprisingly, given that Albion did the double over them, Blues went as well.

SATURDAY 20TH OCTOBER 1888

The inaugural Football League season continued to go well for Albion as they defeated Notts County 4-2 on home soil. Tom Pearson scored two of them, 'Spry' Woodhall and Joe Wilson adding the others; Wilson had already had the honour of scoring Albion's first-ever league goal, at Stoke on the opening day of the campaign.

SATURDAY 20TH OCTOBER 1951

Portsmouth were victims of an on song Albion as the Throstles scored five times without replay at The Hawthorns. Frank Griffin scored twice, Ronnie Allen added a penalty, Arthur Smith weighed in too while Joe Kennedy scored one of just four goals in his 397 appearances for the club.

THURSDAY 20TH OCTOBER 1994

Alan Buckley replaced Keith Burkinshaw as Albion manager after the Baggies had struggled at the start of the season, not least because redevelopment of The Hawthorns meant that the Throstles had to play their first five league games of the season away from home. Buckley had been a prolific goalscorer in the lower divisions with neighbouring Walsall, and had led them to a number of cup successes before building his managerial reputation at Grimsby Town.

SATURDAY 21ST OCTOBER 1978

After Tony Brown was presented with the ball used in the game at Elland Road where he'd broken Ronnie Allen's league goalscoring record, goals were on the menu at The Hawthorns as the Throstles mauled Coventry City 7-1. Laurie Cunningham and Cyrille Regis both scored twice, Len Cantello and Derek Statham were on the scoresheet and the 'Bomber' added another one to his record haul.

TUESDAY 21ST OCTOBER 2003

One of the tiniest away followings in Hawthorns history – counted as 21 diehards – were sent into raptures as struggling Wimbledon scored a late goal after being under the hammer all evening, Jobi McAnuff's goal beating the Baggies 1-0. In the long run, it was of no consequence. At the end of the season, Albion won automatic promotion and Wimbledon were bottom of the pile.

SATURDAY 22ND OCTOBER 1892

The 100th league game in Albion's history was not an occasion for much rejoicing as the Baggies were hammered out of sight by Sunderland, Albion sliding to an 8-1 defeat up on Wearside, Billy Bassett scoring Albion's goal.

SATURDAY 22ND OCTOBER 1910

One of Albion's best club men, Teddy Sandford, was born in Handsworth. As a goalscorer, Sandford played a full part in the 1931 FA Cup and promotion double side, scored in the 1935 FA Cup final defeat to Sheffield Wednesday and later impressed as a defender too. He played 317 games for the Baggies, scoring 75 goals. Later, he ran a cafe very close to The Hawthorns where players and supporters would both congregate. He died in Great Barr in May 1995.

SUNDAY 22ND OCTOBER 2006

Tony Mowbray took charge of an Albion side for the first time and watched them thrash Wolverhampton 3-0. Jonathan Greening, Dio Kamara and a John Hartson penalty gave Albion the first of four wins over the Wolves in a vintage season.

SATURDAY 23RD OCTOBER 1920

Fred Morris won his second and final England cap in the 2-0 win over Ireland at Sunderland's Roker Park, Kelly and Walker scoring for England.

SATURDAY 23RD OCTOBER 1965

Eventual champions Liverpool suffered a rare defeat as an Albion side in top gear won 3-0 at The Hawthorns with goals from Tony Brown, Jon Kaye and Clive Clark.

SATURDAY 23RD OCTOBER 2004

Gary Megson's final game in charge of the Albion ended in disaster as the Baggies were thrashed by a Crystal Palace outfit which ended the season relegated. The home side ran out 3-0 winners, two up inside a dozen minutes. Megson announced in the subsequent days that he did not wish to extend his contract beyond the end of the season and left the club within 48 hours to be replaced by Bryan Robson.

SATURDAY 24TH OCTOBER 1925

Posting their highest score of the season, Albion hammered the Hammers, beating West Ham United 7-1. The goals were shared out with Stan Davies getting a hat-trick, Joe Carter two, 'Tug' Wilson and Tommy Glidden also chipping in. That spread of scorers was the story of the season for Albion where Davies top scored with 19, Wilson scoring 17 and Carter 14.

SATURDAY 24TH OCTOBER 1964

Reigning champions Liverpool were well beaten by Albion, two goals from Clive Clark and another from Jeff Astle seeing the Baggies home 3-0 at The Hawthorns.

SATURDAY 24TH OCTOBER 1987

Tony Morley's hat-trick was instrumental in Albion beating Huddersfield Town, 3-2, at The Hawthorns, crucial points as Albion came within a point of relegation at the end of the campaign.

SATURDAY 25TH OCTOBER 1879

Reputedly the club's first-ever fixture took place against West Bromwich White Hart – a 7-0 victory. Prior to this game coming to light, it was thought the first fixture took place on December 13th 1879, a 1-0 win over Black Lake Victoria.

SATURDAY 25TH OCTOBER 1919

Both Sidney Bowser and Joe Smith made their England debuts in the 1-1 draw with Ireland in Belfast, a game remarkable for the fact that another debutant, Jack Cock, scored after just 30 seconds. The game ended 1-1. Bowser did not play for England again, while Smith won one further cap some four years later. On the same day, their colleagues back at the ranch were busy making light of their absence, beating Notts County 8-0 at The Hawthorns. Fred Morris scored five, Howard Gregory, Tommy Magee and an own goal finished the scoring.

SATURDAY 25TH OCTOBER 1969

Ally Robertson made the first of his 626 appearances for the Baggies, featuring in a 2-1 win over Manchester United in front of 45,120 supporters. Tony Brown and Bobby Hope grabbed the crucial goals.

MONDAY 26TH OCTOBER 1903

With Albion in financial turmoil and the supporters disenchanted, it wasn't the best time to be having a benefit game, but that was the lot that befell Charles 'Chippy' Simmons, whose turn came against Aston Villa. The 3-3 draw saw two goals coming from George Dorsett and the other from Alf Hobson. An estimated crowd of just 5,000 was in attendance.

SATURDAY 26TH OCTOBER 1929

Tommy Glidden was in rare form, scoring four times in the 6-2 home win over Swansea Town, taking his tally to eight goals in four games – ten in seven – Glidden ending the season with a total of 20 goals. Joe Carter and Frank Cresswell finished the rout.

SATURDAY 26TH OCTOBER 1940

Frank Hodgetts became Albion's youngest debutant at 16 years 26 days – and scored to boot – as Albion beat Notts County 3-1 at The Hawthorns. W. G. Richardson scored the other two in a game where Cecil Shaw made his 350th first-class appearance for the Baggies.

SATURDAY 26TH OCTOBER 1957

A typically pulsating encounter with Manchester United saw Albion eventually triumphant as they beat the 'Busby Babes' 4-3 at a packed Hawthorns – 52,839 there to witness the youthful United XI for the last time in the Black Country before the Munich disaster. Bobby Robson twice scored for Albion, Ronnie Allen and Derek Kevan also contributing.

SATURDAY 27TH OCTOBER 1945

Nearing the end of wartime competition, Chelsea visited The Hawthorns only to be thumped 8-1 with four goals coming from Ike Clarke, two from Arthur Rowley and the others from Frank Hodgetts and Doug Witcomb. Albion had been beaten 7-4 at Stamford Bridge a week earlier, Ray Barlow among the goals.

SATURDAY 27TH OCTOBER 1979

Tony Brown blasted in his final Albion penalty as Coventry City were thumped 4-1 at The Hawthorns. 'Bomber' added another goal too. Ally Brown scored two.

SATURDAY 28TH OCTOBER 1922

Tottenham were second best at The Hawthorns as Albion beat them 5-1. Stan Davies got two, John Crisp, Howard Gregory and Ivor Jones notched the rest. Ivor Jones was the father of Cliff Jones who later made his name at White Hart Lane as a brilliant winger and key member of the 1960/61 double winning side.

SATURDAY 28TH OCTOBER 1961

There were goals aplenty at the City Ground as Albion and Nottingham Forest fought out a 4-4 draw with Don Howe, Clive Clark, Derek Kevan and Keith Smith netting. Albion went on to score 14 goals in a four-game sequence.

WEDNESDAY 28TH OCTOBER 1970

The Baggies suffered their worst-ever defeat in the League Cup as Spurs went nap with a 5-0 victory at White Hart Lane in the fourth round tie. Tottenham won the final that year, beating Aston Villa 2-0.

SUNDAY 28TH OCTOBER 2001

On an eventful afternoon in Yorkshire, Albion were beaten 3-2 by Barnsley. Andy Johnson scored his first Albion goal from around 40 yards out while Bob Taylor collected a late red card after an altercation with the opposition goalkeeper.

TUESDAY 29TH OCTOBER 1957

The Hawthorns' new floodlights were officially opened for the visit of the Red Army (CDSA) from the Soviet Union. In an extraordinary evening of entertainment, Albion came out 6-5 winners in front of a huge crowd of 52,805. Derek Kevan scored twice, Ronnie Allen converted a penalty and Bobby Robson, Frank Griffin and Don Howe also scored.

TUESDAY 29TH OCTOBER 1974

Jeff Astle enjoyed his well-deserved testimonial night at The Hawthorns, the crowd a disappointing 11,941 to witness Albion 1974 take on Albion 1968. The 1968 team prevailed 2-1 with goals from Tony Brown and Bobby Hope, Kenny Foggo scoring for the other team. George Best, then on hiatus from Manchester United, was the star turn of the night.

SATURDAY 30TH OCTOBER 1920

Huddersfield Town drew the biggest crowd of the season to The Hawthorns, some 44,049 supporters watching the Throstles come out on top, beating the Terriers 3-0 thanks to Sid Bowser, Joe Smith and Fred Morris. Champions Albion were struggling to find the form of the previous year and this was only their third win some 12 games into the campaign. They ended the season in 14th position.

SATURDAY 30TH OCTOBER 1948

Albion's push for promotion gathered further momentum as they defeated fellow candidates for the top flight, Cardiff City, 2-0 at The Hawthorns. Jack Haines and Cyril Williams were the goalscorers as the Throstles continued a run of a dozen unbeaten games in the league, nine of which were won.

SATURDAY 30TH OCTOBER 1982

Having lost 6-1 to Nottingham Forest earlier in the month, somehow Ron Wylie's Baggies managed to do it again a matter of just 24 days later, this time at Ipswich Town's Portman Road, the scene of a 7-0 trouncing just six years before. Once again it was Cyrille Regis who got the consolation strike for Albion.

WEDNESDAY 30TH OCTOBER 1996

Defender Paul Holmes scored the only goal in his 115 games for the Baggies as his side ran out 3-2 winners away at Swindon Town. Paul Peschisolido and Richard Sneekes were the rather more regular goalscorers who added to Holmes' goal.

SATURDAY 31ST OCTOBER 1970

The reigning champions Everton were sent packing from The Hawthorns as Tony Brown, Jeff Astle and George McVitie posted the goals that saw the Toffees come unstuck, 3-0.

WEDNESDAY 31ST OCTOBER 1973

Willie Johnston registered the first goal of his Albion career when he scored in an otherwise dismal evening at home to Exeter City as the Baggies were bundled out of the League Cup at the third round stage, losing 3-1 to the Grecians.

THE ALBION
On This Day

NOVEMBER

SATURDAY 1st NOVEMBER 1902

Aston Villa were defeated 3-0 at Villa Park, one in a string of six straight wins pieced together by the Throstles in an encouraging start to the season that was later ruined when they ended the campaign with only one win and two draws from the final dozen games to end up seventh in the First Division. Two from John Kifford, and another from Billy Lee, beat the Villa.

WEDNESDAY 1st NOVEMBER 1978

SC Braga pitched up at The Hawthorns for the formality of the Uefa Cup second round second leg tie and were duly put out of their misery by an Ally Brown goal which made the final aggregate score 3-0 to the Throstles.

SATURDAY 1st NOVEMBER 1986

Two goals from Bobby Williamson, added to one from Garth Crooks, saw the Baggies home to a 3-2 derby win over manager Ron Saunders' former club, Birmingham City at The Hawthorns. Crooks ended the season as Albion's top league scorer with 11, despite playing only half the games.

SATURDAY 1st NOVEMBER 2008

In an afternoon of bizarre refereeing decisions, Blackburn Rovers won a dubious penalty and were then surprisingly reduced to ten men as Albion fought back from a goal down to lead 2-1 through Roman Bednar and Ishmael Miller, only to concede a late equaliser to a 25-yard strike in injury time.

WEDNESDAY 2nd NOVEMBER 1966

Albion played in European competition for the first time, taking part in the Inter-Cities Fairs Cup, travelling to take on DOS Utrecht in Holland. The Baggies earned a creditable 1-1 draw out there, Bobby Hope scoring the first goal for the club in Europe.

WEDNESDAY 2nd NOVEMBER 1988

Following a sequence of four straight wins, Brian Talbot was confirmed as permanent player-manager at The Hawthorns, the second man to hold such a role, following in the footsteps of Johnny Giles.

SATURDAY 15TH NOVEMBER 1919

After successive defeats to Notts County and Aston Villa, the Throstles got the show back on the road with a 4-2 victory in the return match at Villa Park, Howard Gregory and Fred Morris getting two goals apiece.

SATURDAY 15TH NOVEMBER 1930

Teddy Sandford played his first game for the Baggies, featuring in the 3-2 win at Preston North End, Sandford scoring at Deepdale, as did Stan Wood and Jimmy Cookson. Within six months Sandford had an FA Cup winner's medal and had helped Albion to promotion.

WEDNESDAY 16TH NOVEMBER 1932

Two years and a day after his club debut, Teddy Sandford collected his only England cap, playing in the goalless draw with Wales at the Racecourse Ground, Wrexham.

WEDNESDAY 16TH NOVEMBER 1960

As the Players' Union debated strike action in order to break the maximum wage structure prevailing in the game, Bobby Robson proclaimed that he did not favour industrial action on that scale. Following a union meeting in Birmingham, Robson said; "I can't afford to go on strike, but I will abide by any union decision." Don Howe, also at the meeting, said he believed that feelings were running increasingly high and that the union was moving towards calling an all-out strike.

SATURDAY 16TH NOVEMBER 1968

Doug Fraser and Asa Hartford were the goalscorers as the Baggies defeated Stoke City at The Hawthorns. To add to the Scottish connection, midfielder Hughie Reed also made his debut for the club.

SATURDAY 16TH NOVEMBER 1991

After the nightmare of defeat against Woking in the FA Cup the previous season, the Baggies were in no mood to be beaten by non-league opposition for a second successive season and were unstoppable in the home tie with Marlow, winning 6-0. Craig Shakespeare scored twice, including a penalty, the rest of the goals came from Gary Strodder, Bernie McNally, Don Goodman and Gary Robson.

TUESDAY 3RD NOVEMBER 1903

Councillor Joseph Round was elected to the Albion's board of directors. This came in the wake of resignations from Harry Keys, Harry Powell and Dr Isaac Pitt.

SATURDAY 3RD NOVEMBER 1956

Albion captain Len Millard played his 600th game for the Albion including wartime appearances etc., and celebrated by playing his part in an emphatic 3-0 victory over Everton at The Hawthorns. Ronnie Allen scored twice, with Bobby Robson getting the other.

SATURDAY 3RD NOVEMBER 2007

A resounding 3-0 win at Vicarage Road, home of runaway Championship leaders Watford changed the very nature of the promotion race, knocking the confidence out of the Hertfordshire outfit, giving the Baggies the belief that was to eventually take them to the title as the Hornets fell down the league to sixth and defeat in the play-offs. Albion's goals came from Ishmael Miller, Kevin Phillips and Martin Albrechtsen.

MONDAY 4TH NOVEMBER 1889

Tom Pearson notched Albion's first ever Football League hat-trick and then went one better by adding a fourth as the Throstles won 6-3 over Bolton Wanderers at Stoney Lane. Billy Bassett and 'Spry' Woodhall completed the scoring for Albion. Pearson added two more hat-tricks before the season was over, giving him a league tally of 17 goals from just 22 games, almost double the total of Albion's next best goalscorer, Jem Bayliss on nine.

SATURDAY 5TH NOVEMBER 1904

Local boy Ted 'Cock' Pheasant made his Albion debut at home to Manchester United as the Baggies fell to a 2-0 defeat. The Darlaston-born Pheasant went on to play 152 games and score 22 goals for Albion.

WEDNESDAY 5TH NOVEMBER 1969

A brace from Jeff Astle proved fireworks enough to defeat Leicester City in a fifth round replay in the League Cup at The Hawthorns, the Baggies making it through to a semi-final meeting with Carlisle United after a 2-1 victory.

SATURDAY 6TH NOVEMBER 1954

Alec Jackson, who had barely been beyond the boundaries of Tipton and West Bromwich before, went down to Charlton Athletic's Valley stadium to make his debut for the Throstles, marking the day with a goal in front of 36,074 fans. Ronnie Allen added two more as Albion were triumphant, 3-1.

SATURDAY 6TH NOVEMBER 1965

Albion were rampant as Fulham visited The Hawthorns only to be thrashed 6-2 by a side that had scored 14 goals in its previous four home fixtures. Both Tony Brown and Graham Lovett helped themselves to two goals each, Clive Clark and Ray Wilson also weighing in, one of only three goals Wilson scored in his 284-game Albion career, two of them coming in his first three games for the club before he was moved from left wing to left-back.

SATURDAY 6TH NOVEMBER 2004

Two goals from Robert Earnshaw, his first goals for the club following a £3 million transfer from Cardiff City, gave the Throstles a 2-2 draw at Southampton in the final game of Frank Burrows' brief reign as Albion's caretaker manager in succession to Gary Megson. It was a vital point as Southampton were relegated at season's end while the Baggies survived, a mere two points ahead of the Saints.

MONDAY 7TH NOVEMBER 1904

Just 48 hours after making his Albion debut, Ted 'Cock' Pheasant banged in his first goal for the Baggies, scoring in the 4-2 win over Blackpool at The Hawthorns. An own goal and others from Henry Aston and Jack Manners sent the northern side packing.

WEDNESDAY 7TH NOVEMBER 2001

Andy Johnson scored with a delightful chip to give the Baggies a 1-0 win over Birmingham City in a game played out in the pouring rain at St. Andrew's. It was to be the final game of Michael Appleton's career. Suspended for Albion's trip to Rotherham United, he then sustained a cruciate injury in training and was never able to sufficiently recover as his rehabilitation went seriously wrong.

SATURDAY 8TH NOVEMBER 1941

Just three weeks after hammering Swansea Town 8-2 at The Hawthorns in the Football League South, Albion managed an even more satisfactory repeat scoreline, this time against Wolverhampton Wanderers at Molineux. Billy Elliott and Charlie Evans helped themselves to hat-tricks, while Jack Sankey and Joe Johnson added the rest. Albion were in a rich vein of goalscoring form at the time, because seven days later, they brought Wolves back to The Hawthorns to administer a 5-3 beating, then on November 21st, they crushed Luton Town 10-1, again at The Hawthorns.

SATURDAY 8TH NOVEMBER 2003

In one of the most remarkable comebacks since Lazarus got out of bed, the Throstles recovered from 3-0 down at West Ham United's Upton Park to win 4-3 with two goals from Rob Hulse, an own goal from Brian Deane, and the winner from Lee Hughes. West Ham's Jermain Defoe helped the cause by getting himself sent off shortly before half-time. A crowd of 30,359 couldn't believe the evidence of their own eyes just seven days after Wolves had performed a similar feat, albeit in rather easier fashion on home soil.

SATURDAY 9TH NOVEMBER 1912

Visitors from London were seen off thanks to two goals from Fred Morris as Albion beat Woolwich Arsenal 2-1. They were relegated at the end of the campaign and weren't able to win promotion back to the top flight before the Great War put a stop to domestic football. When Division One was expanded from 20 to 22 clubs on the resumption, Arsenal, as they were now known, were brought into the fold and have never since been relegated from the top division.

WEDNESDAY 9TH NOVEMBER 1966

The first competitive European fixture ever to be played at The Hawthorns saw the Throstles finish off the job against DOS Utrecht in the Inter-Cities Fairs Cup. After the 1-1 draw in Holland, Albion were ruthless on their own patch and the Dutch side were put to the sword in convincing style, 5-2, Tony Brown registering what remains Albion's only European hat-trick. John Kaye and Clive Clark rounded off the night.

SATURDAY 10TH NOVEMBER 1883

The Albion played their first-ever game in the FA Cup, a 2-0 defeat at Wednesbury Town in the first round. Just two seasons later, Albion would be playing in the FA Cup final itself.

WEDNESDAY 10TH NOVEMBER 1976

Tony Brown broke the league appearance record of 455 games that had stood for more than 50 years, since Jesse Pennington hung up his boots. 'Bomber' played game number 456 against Aston Villa at The Hawthorns and was presented with a silver salver in recognition of the achievement by Albion's chairman, Bert Millichip. The game ended in a 1-1 draw, John Wile scoring for Albion.

SATURDAY 11TH NOVEMBER 1961

Predating the comeback of 2003, Albion reversed a 3-0 deficit at Upton Park to snatch a 3-3 draw with West Ham United, goals from Alec Jackson, Derek Kevan and Don Howe doing the job in front of 18,213 fans.

SATURDAY 11TH NOVEMBER 1967

Goals flowed like water at The Hawthorns as Burnley were smashed out of sight, 8-1, by a rampant Baggies side, with Bobby Hope and Clive Clark scoring twice. Tony Brown, Eddie Colquhoun – his only goal for Albion in 54 games – John Kaye and Jeff Astle were also on the mark.

SATURDAY 11TH NOVEMBER 1989

The biggest win of the season was registered against Barnsley as Albion scored seven times without reply, Don Goodman scoring a hat-trick. Kevin Bartlett added two, Tony Ford and Bernie McNally also joined in the fun.

SATURDAY 11TH NOVEMBER 2006

Albion wore special shirts embroidered with a poppy to commemorate Armistice Day and also to aid the Royal British Legion, the shirts being auctioned off after the game. Norwich City were the visitors to The Hawthorns and despite Albion hitting the woodwork on six separate occasions, they returned to East Anglia with the three points, winning 1-0. The goal came from ex-Albion man Robert Earnshaw.

SATURDAY 12TH NOVEMBER 1892

Accrington were seen off the Stoney Lane premises as Albion posted a comfortable 4-0 win with goals from Roddy McLeod, two from Willie Groves and another from the spectacularly monikered Archibald Middleship Esmond Bastock. The Throstles went up to Accrington for the reserve fixture just over a month later and were beaten 5-4 by the northern side, Bastock getting two goals this time.

SATURDAY 12TH NOVEMBER 1910

Wolves were beaten on home turf once more as the Throstles completed a 3-2 victory with Bobby Pailor scoring twice and Sid Bowser getting the other goal.

SATURDAY 13TH NOVEMBER 1943

In the Football League North, the Baggies beat Stoke City 3-0 at The Hawthorns, W. G. Richardson getting two of his 100 wartime goals for the club, Charles Evans adding the third.

SATURDAY 14TH NOVEMBER 1931

Eighteen-year-old Wally Boyes made his Albion debut in the game against Aston Villa at The Hawhorns, playing his part as goals from W. G. Richardson, Tommy Glidden and Henry Raw saw the Baggies to a 3-0 win over the local enemy. Boyes went on to play 165 games for the Baggies, scoring 38 times, including a goal in the 1935 FA Cup final defeat to Sheffield Wednesday.

SATURDAY 14TH NOVEMBER 1992

Aylesbury became the victims of Albion's biggest ever FA Cup win in the first round of the competition as Ossie Ardiles' side went on the rampage against the non-leaguers. Kevin Donovan scored a hat-trick with Bernie McNally, Bob Taylor, Gary Robson, Paul Raven and Ian Hamilton all getting in on the 8-0 act.

SUNDAY 14TH NOVEMBER 2004

Bryan Robson took charge of the Baggies for the first time as manager, up against previous club Middlesbrough. Albion lost a close game 2-1, the match most memorable for an unbelievable miss by Nwankwo Kanu who somehow put the ball over the bar from two feet out.

SATURDAY 17TH NOVEMBER 1894

Completing a fine week against the occupants of the Second City, the Baggies beat Aston Villa 3-2 at Stoney Lane with goals from Tommy Hutchinson and a couple from Billy Richards. Only seven days earlier, Small Heath had pitched up in West Bromwich and been promptly sent away after losing 4-1, Hutchinson and Richards both scoring. Billy Bassett and Charlie Perry weighed in too.

WEDNESDAY 17TH NOVEMBER 1965

A then record League Cup attendance of 40,694 saw the Baggies stroll past Aston Villa, winning their quarter-final 3-1 at The Hawthorns. Tony Brown maintained his record of scoring in every round, scoring once, John Kaye adding the other two, giving Albion a semi-final appointment with manager Jimmy Hagan's former club, Peterborough United.

SATURDAY 18TH NOVEMBER 1950

Albion completed a 3-2 win at Charlton Athletic with strikes from Fred Richardson, Ronnie Allen and an own goal by Ted Croker, later to become the Secretary of the Football Association.

SATURDAY 18TH NOVEMBER 1961

Derek Kevan continued his free-scoring form for the Albion by knocking in a hat-trick against Sheffield United in a 3-1 win at The Hawthorns. Kevan ended the season with 34 goals in total, the best haul of his career with the Baggies.

SATURDAY 18TH NOVEMBER 1972

Asa Hartford clocked up his 150th league appearance for the Baggies as Albion were beaten 2-0 at Carrow Road by fellow strugglers Norwich City.

SATURDAY 18TH NOVEMBER 2000

Lee Hughes scored a hat-trick as Albion beat Gillingham 3-1 in some comfort at The Hawthorns. Seven days later, Hughes repeated the dose, scoring all three as Preston North End were beaten by the same scoreline. Future Albion player and coach Michael Appleton was sent off for Preston in that game, which also featured another Albion player of the future, Preston captain Sean Gregan.

SATURDAY 19TH NOVEMBER 1898

'Chippy' Simmons made his Albion debut in the Division One fixture up at Burnley. Albion managed a 1-1 draw, Billy Williams scoring for the Baggies. Simmons finished his West Bromwich career with 81 goals from 193 games, and was the first Albion player to score at The Hawthorns.

SATURDAY 19TH NOVEMBER 1955

Graham Williams pulled on the Albion shirt in a senior game for the first time, making his debut in a 2-1 defeat against Blackpool at The Hawthorns. Williams ended up with 360 Albion appearances to his name and has gone down in history as one of the club's finest captains, leading Albion to victory in both the 1966 League Cup and 1968 FA Cup.

SATURDAY 19TH NOVEMBER 2005

The Baggies helped themselves to their biggest Premier League victory by beating Everton 4-0 at The Hawthorns. Nathan Ellington scored twice, his first league goals for the club after his £3 million move from Wigan Athletic. Neil Clement and Robert Earnshaw completed the scoring.

WEDNESDAY 19TH NOVEMBER 2008

Scott Carson became the first Albion player to win an England cap in almost a quarter of a century, coming on as a second-half substitute in the 2-1 win over Germany in the Olympic Stadium in Berlin. Carson's selection between the posts brought to an end a wait of over 24 years for Albion to produce another England international, Steve Hunt being the last back in June 1984.

SATURDAY 20TH NOVEMBER 1897

Goals from Ben Garfield, Albert Flewitt and George Reid saw the Throstles win 3-1 over Derby County at Stoney Lane.

SATURDAY 20TH NOVEMBER 1976

David Cross began the first of two spells at The Hawthorns by making his debut in the 1-0 defeat at Manchester City's Maine Road. Cross had moved across the Midlands in a £140,000 transfer from Coventry City.

SATURDAY 21ST NOVEMBER 1885

On their way to a first-ever FA Cup final at the third time of trying, the Throstles were victorious in a round two fixture against Wednesbury Old Athletic at Stoney Lane, George Bell scoring one, Arthur Loach scoring the others.

SATURDAY 21ST NOVEMBER 1953

Just a few days after England had been humiliated by Hungary, 6-3 at Wembley, Albion showed the country how to play football in the modern era by demolishing Cardiff City 6-1 at The Hawthorns. Ronnie Allen, playing in the deeper lying centre-forward role that was similar to the tactical method used by the Hungarians, picked off four goals, his hat-trick coming inside 30 minutes. Johnnie Nicholls added the other two.

WEDNESDAY 22ND NOVEMBER 1899

In a game redolent of less enlightened times, the Baggies took on a side from South Africa's Orange Free State called the Kaffirs. A mere 1,047 people turned up to see Albion emerge triumphant with an 11-6 victory. Simmons, Reader and Garfield all scored twice. Brett, Paddock, Dwight, Dunn and Walker also scored.

SATURDAY 22ND NOVEMBER 1941

W. G. Richardson scored six goals as Luton Town were beaten 10-1 in a Football League South game at The Hawthorns. Charlie Evans added two, Billy Elliott and Joe Johnson added the others.

SATURDAY 22ND NOVEMBER 1969

Bobby Hope, Jeff Astle and Colin Suggett put their names on the scoresheet as the Baggies recorded a convincing 3-0 win over Sheffield Wednesday, the Owls going on to finish the season bottom of Division One.

WEDNESDAY 22ND NOVEMBER 1978

'Laurie Cunningham's game' was played out in Valencia as the Baggies got a terrific 1-1 draw against a star studded Spanish side that included Mario Kempes, the goalscorer who had led Argentina to the World Cup six months earlier. Cunningham scored Albion's goal and gave an electric performance that essentially sealed his move to Real Madrid.

SATURDAY 23rd NOVEMBER 1878

The *West Bromwich News* reported that West Bromwich Strollers, forerunners of West Bromwich Albion, had organised a 12-a-side game against Hudson's. Many of the players who went on to play for Albion in 1879 were involved in the game, suggesting that the Strollers were involved in organised football prior to 1879, which has led to considerable debate in recent times as to the exact date of Albion's formation.

SATURDAY 23rd NOVEMBER 1968

There was clearly something unpleasant in the dressing room water at Maine Road because after the Baggies had lost the FA Charity Shield curtain-raiser there to the tune of 6-1, a visit for the league game against Manchester City didn't see Albion fare much better, beaten 5-1 with Tony Brown on target for the Throstles. Albion did at least have the consolation of beating them 2-0 at The Hawthorns in the return fixture later in the campaign.

SUNDAY 23rd NOVEMBER 1997

After being penned in by Birmingham City, who missed countless opportunities throughout a tense derby game at The Hawthorns, a late breakaway goal saw Richard Sneekes pinch all three points with the only goal of the game, giving rise to the chant: "We only need one chance!"

SATURDAY 24th NOVEMBER 1923

Bobby Blood's hat-trick led the way as the Throstles saw off the challenge of Everton at The Hawthorns, a 5-0 victory completed by goals from Howard Gregory and Fred Morris.

SATURDAY 24th NOVEMBER 1945

In the final season of wartime league football, Albion trounced Southampton 5-2 in the Football League South, Billy Elliott's hat-trick central to the win. Frank Hodgetts and Arthur Rowley also scored.

SATURDAY 24th NOVEMBER 1984

Albion continued to hold the Indian sign over Coventry City, cruising to a 5-2 win at The Hawthorns with goals from Garry Thompson, Carl Valentine, Steve Mackenzie, Steve Hunt and Derek Statham. Only 12,742 were in attendance.

SATURDAY 25th NOVEMBER 1922

Thomas William Glidden made his Albion debut in the 1-0 win over Everton at Goodison Park, Fred Morris getting the Albion goal. Glidden went on to skipper the Albion, leading the 1930/31 double-winning side and leading the team in the 1935 FA Cup final defeat to Sheffield Wednesday at Wembley. Glidden made 479 appearances and scored 140 goals in his years as an Albion player and, after hanging up his boots, he worked in a coaching capacity at the club, then later was elected to the board of directors. He is remembered to this day in the Glidden Suite in the West Stand of The Hawthorns, while the picture of him holding the FA Cup at Wembley in 1931 is the single most iconic image in Albion history.

SATURDAY 26th NOVEMBER 1921

Stanley Davies made his Albion debut after his transfer from Everton. Davies featured in the 2-0 win against Manchester City at The Hawthorns – goals from Jonathan Blagden and Fred Morris – before going on to make 159 appearances for Albion, scoring 83 goals. Davies was star player for the Welsh national side too, playing 18 games and scoring five times for his country.

SATURDAY 26th NOVEMBER 1955

Maurice Setters made his debut for the Albion in the 1-0 defeat against Huddersfield Town at Leeds Road, having joined the club from Exeter City. Setters, a hard man from the old school, was a real ball winner in midfield, devotee of the 'ask questions later' strain of thought, though initially he was actually an inside-forward at The Hawthorns, scoring twice in his second Albion game against Portsmouth a week later. After 132 appearances for the Throstles, he moved on to Manchester United in 1960 as Matt Busby rebuilt his side post-Munich.

SATURDAY 26th NOVEMBER 1988

While Mark Bright and Ian Wright were a potent striking force for Crystal Palace, they were no match for the Baggies on this day as Albion strode to a 5-3 victory over Steve Coppell's team. Don Goodman underlined his striking credentials with a hat-trick, John Paskin and Robert Hopkins also contributed.

WEDNESDAY 27th NOVEMBER 1957

Bobby Robson marked his England debut in a friendly against France at Wembley by scoring twice in the 4-0 win. Manchester United's Tommy Taylor – later killed in the Munich disaster as were Roger Byrne and Duncan Edwards who also played in this game – got the other two. Don Howe was also in the England side, winning his third cap for his country.

WEDNESDAY 27th NOVEMBER 1968

Romanian opposition was no match for the Baggies as they disposed of Dinamo Bucharest in some style at The Hawthorns, winning 4-0 to complete a 5-1 aggregate win after a stormy 1-1 draw in the Romanian capital where Welsh international winger Ronnie Rees had been sent off. Two goals from Tony Brown and others from Graham Lovett and Jeff Astle saw the Baggies safely into the third round of the European Cup Winners' Cup in front of a crowd of 33,059.

SATURDAY 27th NOVEMBER 1993

In a taxing season where Albion won only 13 games out of 46 in Division One and scored just 60 goals in the process, Portsmouth were always a welcome sight at the opposite end of the field. Pitching up at The Hawthorns, they were on the receiving end of one of only two four-goal hauls dished out by the Baggies, the 4-1 scoreline the joint biggest win of the season. Andy Hunt scored twice, Bob Taylor and Kieran O'Regan helping out with the others for Keith Burkinshaw's team. On the final day of the season, needing to win to survive, Albion went to Fratton Park and won 1-0, completing the third double of the season, the others coming against Watford and Wolverhampton Wanderers.

SATURDAY 28th NOVEMBER 1970

Both John Kaye and Chelsea's Peter Osgood found themselves in hot water with the footballing authorities after the Baggies had played out a 2-2 draw with the Pensioners at The Hawthorns, Colin Suggett and Jeff Astle among the goals. Kaye and Osgood were singled out for reams of press coverage after a post-match spat where Osgood admitted he had deliberately kicked the granite hewn Kaye. Brave man.

SATURDAY 29th NOVEMBER 1913

The game at the centre of a bribery storm was played out to a 1-1 draw by Albion and Everton at The Hawthorns. Prior to the match, Albion's Jesse Pennington had been approached and asked to fix the outcome. Pennington informed the club, and then the police, of the approach, the police asking him to go along with the request as they looked to catch the people involved.

SATURDAY 29th NOVEMBER 1958

Three up at the break, Albion came off best in a seven-goal thriller with Tottenham Hotspur at The Hawthorns. Don Howe, Derek Kevan, Tony Forrester – on his debut – and Ronnie Allen grabbed the goals for the Baggies in front of a crowd of 21,861.

SATURDAY 30th NOVEMBER 1895

James Spooner played his first game for the club, figuring at centre-forward in the 2-0 win over Wolves, Roddy McLeod and Billy Richards scoring the goals. Spooner was said to be a hugely promising player but the club never found out; he suffered a horrible broken leg in his very next game, against Derby County, and was eventually forced to retire from the game.

WEDNESDAY 30th NOVEMBER 1960

The *Daily Herald* reported that nine clubs had threatened to resign from the Football League and create a 'breakaway Super League' as a reaction to the ongoing crisis over the abolition of the maximum wage. Club chairmen were due to meet on December 9th to further discuss the crisis. The paper further reported that, "The club behind the move is believed to be West Bromwich Albion, who have stood out against both the League Cup and television".

SATURDAY 30th NOVEMBER 2002

A goal from Danny Dichio was enough to beat Middlesbrough at The Hawthorns, bringing an end to a run of nine Premier League fixtures without a win under Gary Megson. It was Dichio's first goal of the season but he went on to end the campaign as Albion's top scorer with eight, including a hat-trick against Bradford City in the FA Cup.

THE ALBION
On This Day

DECEMBER

SATURDAY 1st DECEMBER 1888

Albion enter Advent in fine form – opening up gaping holes in the Everton defence – to clinch a thoroughly emphatic 4-1 win; Billy Bassett getting two of them, Billy Hendry and Walter Perry adding the other goals.

SATURDAY 1st DECEMBER 1928

Stalwart defender William Richardson made his Albion debut at Middlesbrough's Ayresome Park, putting in a solid shift in the 1-1 draw as Tommy Glidden scored for the Throstles. Richardson played 352 times for the Baggies, scoring just one goal.

WEDNESDAY 2nd DECEMBER 1998

One of the finest goalkeepers ever to play for the Throstles, John Osborne, passed away after a battle with cancer, the day after his 58th birthday. Ossie was known as the 'bionic man' because of a plastic finger joint, the injury causing him extreme pain in the winter cold, the goalkeeper often having to place his hands in almost boiling water to regain any feeling in them. Osborne joined Albion from Chesterfield in January 1967 and went on to be the Throstles' number one at Wembley in both the 1968 FA Cup final and the League Cup final of two years later, as well as playing in the promotion season of 1975/76. All told, he played 312 games for the club in a distinguished career.

SATURDAY 3rd DECEMBER 1960

Perhaps the greatest English goalscorer of all time chose this day to find his very best form and destroy the Albion in the process. The Baggies went down to a 7-1 thrashing at Chelsea's Stamford Bridge, five of the Chelsea goals coming from the great goal poacher, Jimmy Greaves.

WEDNESDAY 3rd DECEMBER 1969

In front of a packed Hawthorns, the Throstles overturned a 1-0 first leg deficit to defeat Carlisle United 4-1 on the night and advance to the final of the Football League Cup for the third time in five seasons. Bobby Hope, Colin Suggett, Tony Brown and Dennis Martin scored the goals that took the Baggies to Wembley.

SATURDAY 4TH DECEMBER 1926

George 'Cocky' Shaw made his first appearance in Albion colours two days after signing from Huddersfield Town, turning out at Bramall Lane as the Baggies were beaten 2-1 by Sheffield United, George James scoring for Albion. Shaw played in two FA Cup finals, in 1931 and 1935, and played 425 games all told for the club, scoring 11 goals. He had previously been involved in Huddersfield's three consecutive league-winning seasons from 1923/24 onwards, though only as a bit part player, making 24 appearances over the three campaigns.

SATURDAY 5TH DECEMBER 1914

John Crisp made his debut for the Throstles in the final season before World War I closed football down for the duration of the hostilities. Crisp scored in Albion's 2-1 defeat at Everton's Goodison Park. He returned after the war and was an important figure in the side that won the league championship in the first season after the resumption. He ended up by scoring 23 goals for the Baggies in his 124 appearances.

SATURDAY 5TH DECEMBER 1925

Newcastle United made the long trip down to The Hawthorns, but the journey back home to Tyneside must have felt much, much longer as they were undone by an on-song Albion who won 4-0 with two goals from Stan Davies, and one apiece from Charlie 'Tug' Wilson and Arthur 'Mother' Fitton. The latter went on to be coach, and then trainer, at The Hawthorns after the war, accompanying the 1954 FA Cup-winning side to Wembley. All told, Fitton, who was also a very gifted amateur cricketer and played for West Bromwich Dartmouth for many years, spent 18 years at the Albion.

SATURDAY 5TH DECEMBER 1981

Two goals from Cyrille Regis plus another from Clive Whitehead saw the Baggies to a convincing 3-0 win over Wolverhampton Wanderers at The Hawthorns, Albion going on to do the double over the local rivals with a 2-1 win at Molineux later on in the campaign, Regis and Derek Monaghan doing the damage on that occasion. Wolves were relegated at season's end while Albion escaped the dreaded drop by two points.

SATURDAY 6th DECEMBER 1919

On their way to the league title, Albion found their best form as they went to Manchester City and returned home with the two points after completing a narrow 3-2 win, the goals coming from a Sid Bowser penalty and a brace from Fred Morris. A week later, Albion beat Manchester City 2-0 at The Hawthorns, Fred Morris again scoring twice. These fixtures were part of a run of six straight wins, and nine wins in ten games, that broke the back of the competition and put the Throstles firmly in the driving seat in the race for the First Division title.

WEDNESDAY 6th DECEMBER 1978

Albion completed the job they'd started in Valencia by humbling the expensively assembled Spanish giants 2-0 at The Hawthorns to progress to the last eight of the Uefa Cup. Two goals from Tony Brown were crucial in front of 35,118 supporters paying £57,164 for the privilege of being there.

SATURDAY 7th DECEMBER 1963

After scoring five goals in quick succession for the reserves, Micky Fudge was given his chance in the first XI by manager Jimmy Hagan. Fudge saw John Kaye and Clive Clark score the goals as Albion beat Sheffield United 2-0 at The Hawthorns.

SATURDAY 8th DECEMBER 1923

Joe Carter defeated Tottenham Hotspur all but single-handed, sticking four goals in the Londoners' onion bag as his side inflicted a 4-1 defeat on the Lilywhites. The Baggies then went four games without scoring.

SATURDAY 8th DECEMBER 1934

The worst defeat of the season came in a crushing 9-3 beating at the hands of Derby County, goals from W. G. Richardson, Teddy Sandford and Tommy Glidden doing little to make the day any more palatable.

FRIDAY 8th DECEMBER 2000

Jeremy Peace was named as a new director of the club, a post he held until 2002 when he replaced Paul Thompson as the chairman.

SATURDAY 9TH DECEMBER 1911

Claude Jephcott appeared for the Throstles for the first time, in the 3-2 defeat at Sunderland, Bobby Pailor registering the two Albion goals.

SATURDAY 9TH DECEMBER 1922

Joe Carter began his Albion career in unimpressive fashion as the Baggies crashed to a 3-0 defeat at Bolton Wanderers. Despite the early reverse, Carter became an Albion hero, amassing 155 goals in 451 games.

TUESDAY 9TH DECEMBER 1952

Albion manager Jesse Carver left the club to take up a coaching position with Valdagno, after an impressive start to life at The Hawthorns, winning 10 of his 19 games in charge and laying many of the foundations for the way Albion played in the remarkable 1953/54 season.

TUESDAY 9TH DECEMBER 2003

Wreathed in the Yorkshire mists, Scott Dobie found himself in space in the Bradford City area to score the only goal of the game that kept the Throstles on course for promotion back to the Premier League at the first attempt. The game formed part of a sequence of just one defeat in 15 fixtures.

SATURDAY 10TH DECEMBER 1949

Jimmy Dudley, one of the FA Cup winners of 1954, made his Albion debut in the 1-1 draw at Manchester City, Billy Elliott getting the Albion goal. Dudley, a cousin of Jimmy Edwards from the 1931 FA Cup winners, played 320 games and scored 11 goals in total for the Throstles.

TUESDAY 10TH DECEMBER 1963

Trouble broke out in the form of a players' revolt as ten members of the first team squad went on strike in protest at manager Jimmy Hagan's training methods, and his refusal to allow the players to wear tracksuits in the icy weather. Ray Potter, Don Howe, Graham Williams, Doug Fraser, Stan Jones, John Kaye, Bobby Hope, Ronnie Fenton, Terry Simpson – who had played for Hagan at Peterborough United – and Clive Clark put in a mass transfer request.

SATURDAY 11TH DECEMBER 1948

Cyril Williams produced a hat-trick, the only one of his Albion career, to spearhead a 5-2 win over Grimsby Town at The Hawthorns in the promotion-winning season. Jack Haines added one from the spot while Dave Walsh also got himself on the scoresheet.

SATURDAY 11TH DECEMBER 1954

Goalkeeper Jim Sanders posted his 250th appearance for the Baggies, but there was little else to celebrate as he finished up on the losing side, as Albion were beaten by Blackpool by the only goal of the game. At least it was better than his 249th game for the club. The week before, Sanders had fished the ball out of the net six times as the Baggies were thrashed 6-1 at Portsmouth's Fratton Park.

SATURDAY 11TH DECEMBER 1982

Sunderland were decidedly second best at The Hawthorns as Albion romped to a 3-0 victory. Dutch midfielder Romeo Zondervan scored his first goal for the club, Gary Owen chipped in too, as did Alistair Robertson. Robertson scored just a dozen goals in a massive 626 games for the Baggies, yet the Sunderland goal was his second in three games having scored against Coventry City in a 2-0 win a fortnight earlier.

SATURDAY 12TH DECEMBER 1914

Goals from Claude Jephcott and Arthur Swift were enough to see Albion to a 2-0 win over Chelsea at The Hawthorns.

SATURDAY 12TH DECEMBER 1931

A good day to be playing Chelsea as the Londoners slumped to a 4-0 defeat this time; W. G. Richardson's brace was added to by Wally Boyes and Tommy Glidden. The Baggies were going well as they approached Christmas in their first season back in the big time, and they ended the season in sixth place.

SATURDAY 12TH DECEMBER 1970

Tony Brown bagged himself a pre-Christmas hat-trick as Albion were comfortable winners against Tottenham Hotspur at The Hawthorns, 3-1 the final score.

ALISTAIR ROBERTSON SCORED A RARE GOAL FOR ALBION AGAINST SUNDERLAND ON 11TH DECEMBER 1982

SATURDAY 13TH DECEMBER 1924

Nottingham Forest were on the receiving end of the wrath of George James, in the midst of a hot streak of goalscoring form. James stuck four past the hapless Forest defence, Joe Carter adding another to round out a 5-1 win. James scored 13 goals in a seven-game period through December and into the beginning of 1925.

SATURDAY 13TH DECEMBER 1947

After playing 35 wartime games for the Baggies, Norman Heath made his 'official' debut for the club in the 2-1 win at Hillsborough, Dave Walsh and Billy Elliott getting the goals that were too much for Sheffield Wednesday.

SATURDAY 13TH DECEMBER 1952

Jimmy Dugdale, who won FA Cup winner's medals with both Albion and Aston Villa inside three years, made his debut for the Throstles in a 1-0 defeat at Bolton Wanderers, Dugdale winning plenty of plaudits for the way he handled Bolton's great striker, Nat Lofthouse.

SATURDAY 13TH DECEMBER 1969

Jeff Astle was the difference between the two sides as Albion edged to a 1-0 victory at Ipswich Town. Astle was on his way to topping the scoring charts with 30 goals ahead of the World Cup.

SATURDAY 14TH DECEMBER 1963

Amid the ongoing dispute with players at The Hawthorns, they put their problems to one side to take on Leicester City at Filbert Street, Kenny Foggo and one of the rebels, Doug Fraser, seeing Albion to a 2-0 victory.

TUESDAY 14TH DECEMBER 1999

As the Baggies were travelling to a game at Grimsby Town, winger Kevin Kilbane was sold to Sunderland for £2.5 million, manager Brian Little allegedly not learning of the decision until the team got off the coach. The sale of Kilbane, in prime form, sparked widespread anger amongst supporters and began the train of events that saw Tony Hale step down as chairman three days later, ultimately to be replaced by Paul Thompson.

SATURDAY 15TH DECEMBER 1962

Manchester United were put to the sword in no uncertain fashion as the Baggies carved them up, 3-0 at The Hawthorns. Bobby Cram scored his first Albion goal to add to others by Keith Smith and Alec Jackson as Matt Busby's team were defeated.

WEDNESDAY 15TH DECEMBER 1965

At Peterborough United's London Road ground, defending a slim 2-1 lead from the first leg of the semi-final, Albion advanced imperiously into the final with West Ham United by beating the Posh 4-2, a Tony Brown hat-trick instrumental in the win, Ray Crawford adding the other goal to complete a 6-3 aggregate victory. By the time the final itself came around almost three months later, Crawford had left the Baggies, rejoining Ipswich Town where he had earlier won a league title under Alf Ramsey.

SATURDAY 15TH DECEMBER 2007

A see-saw afternoon at The Hawthorns saw the Baggies triumph in the finish, beating newly relegated Charlton Athletic 4-2, two goals from Zoltan Gera and others from Roman Bednar and Kevin Phillips doing the trick against the Addicks.

SATURDAY 16TH DECEMBER 1911

Eventual champions Blackburn Rovers didn't lose many games in the 1911/2 season, but they were beaten on this day at The Hawthorns as Sid Bowser and Bob Pailor inflicted the punishment on them, Albion keeping a clean sheet at the other end.

SATURDAY 16TH DECEMBER 1972

Asa Hartford played the 200th senior game of his Albion career in a 2-1 defeat at Highbury, Tony Brown getting the consolation strike against Arsenal.

SATURDAY 16TH DECEMBER 1978

The triumphant 1978/79 season continued unchecked as Albion went to Molineux and hammered Wolves 3-0, Ally Brown getting two of the goals, Tony Brown the other. This was the second in a sequence of five straight wins – eight out of nine – in Division One as the Baggies pushed for top spot.

SATURDAY 17TH DECEMBER 1927

Harold Pearson made his debut as Albion's goalkeeper in the 3-0 win over South Shields at The Hawthorns, thereby following in the footsteps of his father Hubert who had been a part of the league championship-winning side of 1919/20. Harold went on to win the FA Cup and play for England, completing the Pearson family's set of medals and honours.

SATURDAY 18TH DECEMBER 1976

One of the most skilful players ever to represent the Throstles, left-back Derek Statham made his debut at Stoke City's Victoria Ground and announced the arrival of a major talent by scoring in the 2-0 victory, John Trewick getting the other goal. Statham played 378 games for the club, scoring 10 times.

SUNDAY 18TH DECEMBER 1988

Another Albion victory over the Potters, and this one could hardly have been any more emphatic as Stoke City were thrashed 6-0 at The Hawthorns. Three Albion men, Don Goodman, John Paskin and Gary Robson, helped themselves to two goals apiece as the Throstles began to threaten a real run at promotion under Brian Talbot.

SATURDAY 18TH DECEMBER 1999

Albion's troubles went from bad to worse as they were well beaten, 3-1 at Ipswich Town, ending up with only nine men after Larus Sigurdsson and Matt Carbon were sent off. On top of that, Alan Miller and Paul Raven were then involved in a brawl in the tunnel and had to be separated, Brian Little calling for calm in the aftermath of it all as Albion hurtled towards the lower reaches of the division.

SATURDAY 18TH DECEMBER 2004

Misery piled upon misery as the Throstles were humiliated at St. Andrew's, Birmingham City winning 4-0, as plenty of Albion supporters headed off at half-time with the game already lost to do some Christmas shopping instead. It left the Albion bottom of the Premier League at Christmas and seemingly doomed to relegation after chalking up a seventh defeat in nine games, yet somehow, they pulled off the 'Great Escape' to survive.

SATURDAY 19TH DECEMBER 1925

According to the club tape measure, Manchester United were thrashed within an inch of their lives at The Hawthorns, 5-1 the final score before a poor pre-Christmas crowd of 16,554. Stan Davies scored twice, Tommy Glidden, Joe Carter and 'Tug' Wilson scoring the other three. The United win was part of a massive goalscoring spree in the Black Country that saw the Throstles register 32 goals in seven home games.

SATURDAY 19TH DECEMBER 1959

Manchester United fell victim to the Baggies once again, this time up at Old Trafford. Derek Hogg, Ronnie Allen and David Burnside scored the goals that mattered in a 3-2 win.

THURSDAY 19TH DECEMBER 1963

Nineteen players walked out of training at the Spring Road training ground in further protest at Jimmy Hagan's methods in the pre-Christmas freeze. The revolt was eventually quelled when the players were allowed to train inside, in the gymnasium, at Spring Road.

SATURDAY 19TH DECEMBER 1970

John Wile played the first of his 619 games for the Throstles after his move from Peterborough United, featuring in the 1-1 draw with Blackpool. Colin Suggett scored for Albion.

SATURDAY 20TH DECEMBER 1930

The Throstles made a decisive move towards promotion by defeating Stoke City, 4-0 at The Hawthorns, bouncing back from a damaging defeat at Bradford Park Avenue. W. G. Richardson and Tommy Magee were on target as was skipper Tommy Glidden who scored two.

SATURDAY 20TH DECEMBER 1958

Albion's home game with Luton Town had to be abandoned because of torrential rain with the two teams locked at 1-1, Don Howe having scored the goal for the Baggies. The rearranged game didn't take place until April 15th 1959, Albion winning 2-0 as Luton prepared for the upcoming FA Cup final with Nottingham Forest. Ronnie Allen and David Burnside scored the goals that secured victory.

SATURDAY 21st DECEMBER 1974

The highest Hawthorns crowd of the season, 29,614, was treated to some fine Christmas fare as the Throstles beat Aston Villa 2-0 with goals from Willie Johnston and Joe Mayo.

THURSDAY 22nd DECEMBER 1938

Billy Elliott signed for the Albion at Bournemouth's Dean Court ground, Albion club secretary Fred Everiss heading down to the south coast in order to do the necessary paperwork. Within two days, Elliott was in the Albion side, making his debut in the 3-1 defeat to Luton Town on Christmas Eve. The winger played 303 Albion games in total, either side of World War II, scoring 157 goals. Elliott also represented England in two wartime internationals.

THURSDAY 22nd DECEMBER 1977

Ronnie Allen tendered his resignation as Albion manager after just six months at the helm, tempted away by a lucrative coaching offer from Kuwait. He eventually returned to the club, taking over as first-team boss for the second time after Ron Atkinson left for Manchester United in 1981.

FRIDAY 23rd DECEMBER 1966

Graham Lovett was seriously injured in a terrible car crash on the M1 when his car went down an embankment, leaving him trapped for several hours before he was discovered and taken to hospital. He didn't return to the first team until Boxing Day in 1967 when he made an appearance as substitute in the 3-2 win over Manchester City, though in truth, he was lucky ever to play again given the severity of his injuries.

SATURDAY 23rd DECEMBER 1972

A mere 12,059, the lowest gate of the season, were in attendance at The Hawthorns as John Wile made his 100th first-team appearance in the 2-0 home win over Ipswich Town, courtesy of goals from Allan Glover and Asa Hartford.

FRIDAY 23rd DECEMBER 1977

John Wile was appointed caretaker manager of the Baggies after Ronnie Allen's defection to Kuwait.

SATURDAY 24th DECEMBER 1932

Albion and Leicester City set everyone up for Christmas with a cracking game at The Hawthorns, the Throstles eventually prevailing 4-3, Teddy Sandford adding a goal to the hat-trick scored by W. G. Richardson. Richardson clearly enjoyed the festive season because he repeated the dose on Boxing Day, smacking three past Sunderland in the 5-1 win.

WEDNESDAY 24th DECEMBER 1997

After Ray Harford had walked out on Albion to go to Queens Park Rangers, Denis Smith was appointed the new manager of the club, a position he held for the next 74 games before he was dismissed on the eve of the 1999/2000 season. Smith's first game in charge was at Reading's Elm Park on Boxing Day, losing 2-1, Kevin Kilbane the scorer.

THURSDAY 25th DECEMBER 1914

As British and German troops observed an informal ceasefire and played a game of football in no-man's-land near Armentieres in France, the Baggies played an altogether safer fixture at Turf Moor, Burnley, coming out 2-0 winners through Fred Morris and Arthur Swift.

SATURDAY 25th DECEMBER 1948

Jack Vernon scored the only goal of his distinguished Albion career, and the only goal of the game too, as the Throstles enjoyed Christmas Day by defeating Sheffield Wednesday at The Hawthorns. 1949 proved to be a happy new year, the Baggies going on to win promotion.

FRIDAY 25th DECEMBER 1953

Albion's superb season continued in full swing as they defeated Liverpool 5-2 at The Hawthorns with two from Frank Griffin, and others from Ray Barlow, Johnnie Nicholls and Ronnie Allen.

TUESDAY 25th DECEMBER 1956

The last-ever Christmas Day game to feature the Albion saw them defeat Newcastle United by a single Ray Barlow goal. There was little time for Christmas dinner afterwards as both teams set out for Tyneside and a repeat fixture the following day, the Throstles defeated 5-2.

THURSDAY 26TH DECEMBER 1929

A 6-1 win over Millwall made for a very enjoyable Boxing Day for 24,032 in The Hawthorns, Joe Carter and Tommy Glidden scoring twice, Stan Wood adding another and W. G. Richardson crowning his debut with a goal too.

FRIDAY 26TH DECEMBER 1952

An enthralling game at Hillsborough saw Sheffield Wednesday twice put the ball in their own net as the Baggies ran out 5-4 winners, the other goals coming from Ray Barlow, Ronnie Allen and Johnnie Nicholls. The following day, the opposite fixture took place at The Hawthorns, Albion losing 1-0.

TUESDAY 26TH DECEMBER 1961

A poor Christmas crowd of only 24,778 at The Hawthorns saw Albion share a 1-1 draw with Wolves, Derek Kevan scoring for the home side, one of 34 goals he tanked in that season.

THURSDAY 26TH DECEMBER 1963

Another Christmas cracker ended 4-4 between Albion and Tottenham Hotspur at The Hawthorns, John Kaye, Clive Clark, Micky Fudge and Don Howe all on target. Spurs were regular festive opposition at the time and three years to the day later, they were beaten 3-0 by a Tony Brown hat-trick.

MONDAY 26TH DECEMBER 1994

At the official reopening of the new all-seater Hawthorns, the Throstles edged to a somewhat fortuitous win over Bristol City, courtesy of a scruffy Munro own goal, ensuring that just as when the original Hawthorns opened in 1900, the first goal at the redeveloped stadium was scored by an opposition player – albeit for Albion this time.

WEDNESDAY 26TH DECEMBER 2007

Hitting top form for Christmas, Albion swept aside the challenge of Bristol City with a powerful second-half display in which Roman Bednar, Robert Koren and then two from Kevin Phillips saw them home to a 4-1 win over their promotion rivals. Three days later, they thumped Scunthorpe United 5-0 to stay on course for the Premier League.

WEDNESDAY 27TH DECEMBER 1893

Now that's what I call a Christmas present. Wolverhampton were destroyed at Molineux as the Throstles knocked in eight goals without reply to take the points. Roddy McLeod got a hat-trick, Billy Bassett did likewise and Charlie Perry and Owen Williams, making his debut, shared the others.

SATURDAY 27TH DECEMBER 1919

Albion enjoyed a Christmas double of back-to-back home games, the double completed with a 3-0 win over Derby County on this day after Sunderland were defeated 4-0 the day before. A remarkable 77,656 fans attended the two games in which Fred Morris scored four goals, Tommy Magee two and Alf Bentley one as the Throstles chased a first league title.

SATURDAY 28TH DECEMBER 1929

Wolves were beaten 7-3 in very convincing fashion at The Hawthorns, an own goal adding to two from Frank Cresswell and Joe Carter, and others from Tommy Glidden and Joe Evans.

SATURDAY 28TH DECEMBER 1957

Bobby Robson completed a very satisfactory Christmas for himself and for his club, scoring four in the 5-1 win over Burnley at The Hawthorns, Derek Kevan chiming in with the other strike. Robson had scored two – as had Kevan – on Boxing Day when Albion won 5-3 at St. Andrew's, Ronnie Allen getting the other goal in the beating of the Blues.

SATURDAY 28TH DECEMBER 1996

The Baggies made it 12 goals in three games at The Hawthorns by trouncing Queens Park Rangers 4-1, the goals shared out between Richard Sneekes, Andy Hunt, Paul Peschisolido and David Smith, one of just two goals he scored in 117 games.

TUESDAY 28TH DECEMBER 2004

After being reduced to ten men following Thomas Gaardsoe's dismissal and immediately going behind at the City of Manchester Stadium, the Baggies somehow engineered a 1-1 draw against Manchester City without having a shot at goal, the equaliser coming courtesy of a Richard Dunne own goal.

SATURDAY 29TH DECEMBER 1888

Stoke City were no match for the Baggies who won 2-0 at Stoney Lane to complete the double over them in the first season of the Football League. Billy Bassett and Joe Wilson were the scorers.

SATURDAY 29TH DECEMBER 1928

Clapton Orient were beaten on home turf by an Albion side unbeaten in eight games, Jimmy Cookson and Tommy Glidden on target in front of just 6,400 fans.

SATURDAY 30TH DECEMBER 1967

The Throstles completed the double over Manchester City by beating them twice inside four days. After winning 3-2 at The Hawthorns, Albion earned an even better result up at Maine Road, Dick Krzywicki and Tony Brown clinching a 2-0 win over the eventual First Division winners.

SATURDAY 30TH DECEMBER 1978

One of the most famous Christmas games of all time, the Throstles went up to Old Trafford and won 5-3 in a game fortunately caught for posterity by the television cameras. A thrilling game went from end to end but Albion came out on top thanks to two from Tony Brown, the Goal of the Season from Len Cantello, and other crackers from Laurie Cunningham and Cyrille Regis. Had the United goalkeeper Gary Bailey not been in such outstanding form, the scoreline could have been even greater, but the fact that Tony Brown scored past him meant that he completed the rare double of scoring goals past father and son – he scored past Gary's dad Roy when he played for Ipswich in the 1960s.

SATURDAY 31ST DECEMBER 1932

The final day of 1932 offered up a fine win over Everton as the Baggies won 2-1 at Goodison Park with goals from Tommy Glidden and Walter Robbins.

SATURDAY 31ST DECEMBER 1994

Andy Hunt's goal was sufficient to beat Bolton Wanderers at The Hawthorns as Alan Buckley's team completed a vital 1-0 win over a team including one Richard Sneekes.